12 DAYS of CHRISTMAS

Recovering a season of giving, feasting, & reflection

BY CHRIS & GLENCORA PIPKIN

Twelve Tide: 12 Days of Christmas, Recovering a season of giving, feasting, and reflection
Copyright © 2023 by Chris Pipkin and Glencora Pipkin
www.12tide.com

ISBN: 9798863824819
Imprint: Independently published

Printed in the United States of America.

CONTENTS

DEDICATION

To our children,
Davey, Virginia, Adriana, and Arthur:
May God grant you open hands and steadfast hearts.

ACKNOWLEDGMENTS

Thank you to **our children**—Davey, Virginia, Adriana, and Arthur—for being the inspiration for this work.

Thank you to our **faithful Twelve Tide blog readers,** who have encouraged our efforts in sharing our creation.

Thank you to **Christine Cowan** for editing and proofing the manuscript.

Thank you to **Fr. Daniel Adkinson**, who so happily shared our efforts with others. Thank you to our community at St. Thomas Church in Athens, GA.

Thank you to **Donna and David Pipkin**, who have watched our children countless hours to help us complete this book.

Thank you to **Father, Son, and Holy Spirit**, who have guided our hearts and hands. To God be the glory!

INTRODUCTION

We were new parents when we decided to start celebrating Christmas over twelve days rather than one.

This was, first, a practical decision rather than anything pious or romantic. We don't even really like the song about all the pear trees, milkmaids, and golden rings.

We'd simply been stressed in the week leading up to December 25. We felt an enormous amount of pressure to buy "enough" gifts for each other and our loved ones, so that no one would have a disappointing Christmas. We were also aware that, as magical (and insomnia-inducing) as it is for kids to see thirty wrapped gifts under a tree, it means that only one or two new gifts will be appreciated and enjoyed, and that small children are prone to over-stimulation and meltdown.

I'm not sure how it happened, exactly (early parenthood is one big memory-hole), but at some point one of us must have turned to the other and said, "You know, people used to celebrate Christmas for much longer. What if we spaced our gifts out a bit between Christmas Eve and Epiphany?"

That was (I'm guessing) Christmas of 2015. After a few years, rather than having regrets, we found more reasons to continue celebrating Christmas this way.

For one thing, the last-minute stress of Christmas Eve is mostly gone, replaced with excitement and enjoyment of each other and the season. We can purchase gifts after December 24, often at lower cost. We don't have to bite our nails over whether a gift we've ordered will arrive in time.

More importantly, as our kids have gotten older, we've wrapped the giving of each day's gift in a kind of ceremony. We are Christian, and we use this season to mark the birth of God into the world as a human being. Doing this over the course of twelve days (usually at a set time each day) gives us more time to meditate together on the significance of Jesus' Incarnation. We usually read Scripture together, say a prayer, and teach our kids a Christmas Carol, which becomes the "Carol of the Day."

It seemed likely to us that this sort of practice could be easily adopted by other families, couples, individuals, communities, or groups of friends. So a few years ago, we started a site called 12tide.com because we wanted to help transform how Christmas is celebrated in our culture. Over the years, it has been gratifying and humbling to hear that others have enjoyed and used the site.

We've long planned to turn the site into a book (partly to reduce the role of screens in Christmas celebrations and partly because books are nice), and we'd like to encourage you to add to your own practice of Christmas the traditions and ideas that seem like a good fit for you, your family, and community. The following pages feature prayers, reflections, suggested gifts, journal prompts, activities, and carols, as well as excerpts from literature for each day.

We really do believe that this method of celebrating Christmas enhances the joy and meaning already present in this season, elevating the practice of reflection and gift-giving, while reducing stress and consumerism. At the same time, of course, we recognize that this is not the only way to enjoy Christmas; the twelve-day model gives us a framework upon which we can improvise. The following pages hold ideas we've either come up with or inherited from older traditions.

—The Pipkins

HOW TO USE THIS BOOK

First, flip through the book a bit to get an idea of what you're getting yourself into. Read some of the ideas for gift-giving and activities ahead of time, as some of the suggestions can involve a bit of planning ahead.

Also, if you are going to celebrate twelve days of Christmas, it is probably wise to make Advent (traditionally from December 1-24) a time of reflection and fasting. Feel free to look on our site (www.12tide. com) for additional Advent resources and reflections. Do what you can to make most of December a time of fasting, good works, and meditation, perhaps even resisting carols and confections where possible. The darkness of Advent allows the light of Christmas to shine even more brightly as it approaches.

This book is one vision of how your Christmas could be celebrated as a twelve-day season. The practices included here have enhanced our own Christmas each year, and we wanted to share them with others. This is not anything commanded by God or the authority of any church. It's not meant to be an absolute answer to your existential Christmas problems.

In other words, I would not advise trying to do everything suggested in this book each year. We certainly don't. Instead, take what works for you (and your family/community) and leave the rest for future years. Hopefully the book is something you can return to during successive Christmases, adding your own traditions to it as you do. We hope the ideas in this book inspire you to celebrate Christmas more creatively and traditionally. May this help release you from consumerist legalism, rather than giving you a new set of rules to follow. Rest and rejoice.

We tend to use the material in this book before and after we open presents on each day of Christmas. We'll pray the day's prayer, read the suggested scriptures and teach our children one of the carols of the day. Then (at last) we open presents. Later, we do one or two of the activities suggested. We'll usually read the reflections and literature on our own, at night or in the morning, though we'll probably introduce these to our older kids soon.

The book is divided into sections that correspond with the

traditional twelve days of Christmas. These begin on the evening of December 24 and end with Epiphany (so we have fourteen sections rather than twelve). Most are themed around a saint or event (such as Christ's naming) traditionally celebrated that day. Occasionally there is no traditional saint or event celebrated, and in these cases, we have more general thoughts and traditions having to do with an aspect of Christmas, such as community or gift-giving.

Each day includes the following sub-sections:

Prayers for the day. These are taken from the public domain version of the Book of Common Prayer. If you come from a liturgical church, by all means, replace these with your own church's recommended prayers for that day. We believe that scripted prayers, rather than being inauthentic, can actually help you meditate on aspects of God you wouldn't naturally think about on your own—just as scripted songs can. But feel free to wing it as well. Above all, pray.

Reflections. These are devotionals or meditations written by the us, often in response to either the occasion or saint celebrated on a given day or in response to relevant Scripture. By the way, there are more of these up on the site (www.12tide.com) during Advent—the month of fasting that precedes Christmas.

Giving. There are a few ideas in this section for types of gifts you can give on a certain day. Some of the suggestions are in keeping with the day's saint or theme, while others are not. We really do recommend giving gifts throughout the Christmas season if possible, but we are very aware of the fact that we certainly don't have twelve gifts for each person in our family. Because of this, we've included a "No-Cash Option" to get you thinking creatively about how you can still give to someone else without breaking the bank or resorting to buying cheap junk. In lieu of a gift, by the way, we sometimes do something special, which brings us to the next section...

Activities. We've included old traditions here from the deeps of time and various parts of the world, as well as (sometimes weird) new ideas that have been meaningful to us. Feel free to write your own recovered or invented traditions in the margins so that you remember them the next year.

Literature. Okay, we like to read. And Christmas is a great time to sit down with a poem or a piece of fiction and just allow yourself to soak it in. Some of the literature here is explicitly religious, and some is not at all—which seems, to us, quite appropriate for Christmas. We would have included more if we could. The fiction we excerpt is easy enough to find online (or in book form) if you want to read more. Everything is public domain, except for a poem Chris wrote at the very end (mostly because we couldn't find something for Epiphany that wasn't under copyright).

Scripture. This is a brief section, but a lot of thought went into finding passages of Scripture that have something to do with each day's theme. If your tradition already has scripture assigned to specific days, though, we encourage you to follow that.

Carol of the Day. Another brief section (in the book) that is quite important to us. We try to use the twelve days of Christmas to teach our children fourteen different carols (at least the first verse and chorus). For each day, we've suggested two carols to choose from. Feel free to look up the lyrics on our site (www.12tide.com) if you'd like. The page should have a video with the music as well. Some of the carols listed here (such as The Boar's Head Carol and the Coventry Carol) have become less familiar in recent centuries and are well worth recovering. Others have been around since at least the nineteenth century and continue to be Christmas staples.

Journal Prompts. This section prompts you to respond to the scripture, reflection, and literature. If you're not the journal-writing kind, feel free to simply discuss these questions with your family or community.

Finally, we've included space at the end of the book for you to write your own Christmas ideas and traditions. We do encourage you to annotate and write down ideas in this book. Far from ruining it, this marks it as your own and allows you to adapt it to whatever God is doing in you and among your family from one Christmas to the next.

Joyeux Noel,
The Pipkins

Christmas Eve

O God, who has caused this holy night to shine with the illumination of the true Light: Grant us, we beseech you, that as we have known the mystery of that Light upon earth, so may we also perfectly enjoy him in heaven; where with you and the Holy Spirit he lives and reigns, one God, in glory everlasting. Amen.

—*The Book of Common Prayer*

REFLECTION

Christmas predates Christ. We have all heard this. No one is sure when Jesus was actually born, yet the Christian Church has traditionally celebrated his birth at the darkest time of the year. Cynics view this tradition as a way that the Church co-opted pagan holidays like Saturnalia or Yule for its own purposes. The Christian counter-explanation is that, regardless of when Jesus was actually born, the symbolism is the most important thing: that when everything was cold and dark, Christ, the true light, entered the world. This idea certainly resonates with me: The contrast between the light and darkness of the year is pleasurable, as is the juxtaposition of cold and heat. If Christ is the Light of the World, he is brightest when darkness is most pervasive.

Yet even the view that Christmas is an airbrushed pagan holiday can give us a certain amount of insight into the nature of a God who becomes human, entering our culture from the inside and sanctifying it.

What else should we expect from "Jesus, our Emmanuel," who is, as the old song says, "Pleased as man with men to dwell"?

Which brings us to another myth that may be worth exploding: Just because he was laid in a manger doesn't mean Jesus was born in a stable. Everyone kept animals, and everyone had mangers, often in their bedrooms. Homes were composed of two rooms: a nice inner room for guests, where family from out of town stayed, and an outer room for members of the host family—including their animals. The word translated "inn" in Luke 2 probably means "guest room." Just because Jesus was laid in some poor animal's food trough does not mean he was born on the edges of town in some remote stable.

On the contrary, while he is surely Holy, surely Other, surely Miraculous, he is also part of the noise, bother, and disruption of humanity. There may not have been space within the inner room for yet another relative, but he made his dwelling with people. This fact is paralleled by the story of the shepherds—consummate outsiders whose otherworldly encounter with angels draws them not to further ecstatic mountaintop experiences but rather toward the homely lights of Bethlehem to see a seemingly ordinary human child.

ACTIVITIES

- Have dinner together and go to your church's service.
- Go to an evening church service in a denomination you're not familiar with.
- Watch a Christmas special together on television and drink something warm. Discuss what the special got right about Christmas and what it got wrong.
- Listen to Handel's "Messiah" or go to a performance of it.

- Listen to an old-timey radio Christmas special.
- Go caroling with friends or family.
- Wait and watch for the first star to appear in the sky. When it does, begin Christmas dinner. Spend the rest of the evening telling stories around the fire.
- In much of Europe, it is traditional to eat fish for Christmas Eve dinner and to wait until after midnight mass to eat other types of food.
- Talk with an older relative about how they or their parents grew up celebrating Christmas, and recover that tradition (this may, of course, take some planning ahead of time).

GIFT GIVING

- A small purchased gift.
- If you've gotten pajamas, slippers, or a stuffed animal for someone, now might be the time to give it to them (although if your child expects to unwrap a toy, they may be upset, a lesson we learned the hard way). We typically give pajamas on Christmas Eve and then read the nativity story before bed. Our children know that at whatever time they wake up on Christmas morning, their stockings will be at the foot of their beds.
- NO CASH OPTION: Write a Christmas carol or short poem featuring a loved one, illustrate it, and give it to them.

Sensieut loroison du glorieux sait anthome
faute par le translatteur /

esyglorieux en grande de merite /
Samt anthome / qaux desers decript

sluz manoix fupant mondaine
Laiffant la char qui en mal se delite
Tout tapluas pour auoir ioie eslite
Qui sane fin dure a perpetuite
Tant mespusas mondaine baute

LITERATURE

An excerpt from *Sir Gawain and the Green Knight,*
translated by Chris Pipkin

In this fourteenth-century poem, the famous Sir Gawain is searching for a strange and enormous Green Knight. He promised last Christmas to allow the Knight to strike his head off—and he always keeps his promises. He has said farewell to Arthur's Court at Camelot and is passing through the inhospitable wilderness as he searches for death. As Christmas approaches, Gawain becomes anxious that he will not be able to attend Christmas Eve Mass. This translation begins in the midst of a description of the wild men (woodwoses) and wild animals (including "Worms," or dragons) Gawain must fight in the wilderness, as well as the (far deadlier) cold.

Somewhile with Worms he wars and with wolves also,

somewhile with woodwoses that dwelt in the rocks,

both with bulls and bears, and boars elsewhile,

and trolls that tramped down from the high hill.

Had he not been steadfast and served the Savior,

doubtless he would have been driven to his death.

For war worried him not so much as winter (far worse!),

when the cold clear water from the clouds was shed

and froze 'ere it could fall to the faded earth.

Near slain with the sleet, he slept in his armor

more nights than enough, between naked rocks

while once-clamorous waters that ran from the crest

now hung high over his head in hard icicles.

Thus in peril and pain and plights full hard

through country comes this knight until Christmas Eve,

alone.

The knight well at that tide

to Mary made his moan:

That she would kindly guide

and bring him to some home.

By a mount on that morning the man rides

into a deep wood that was wild and weird,

high hills on each side, and under woods

of hoary oaks full huge, a hundred together;

The hazel and the hawthorn were all thus entwined,

with rough ragged moss that ran everywhere,

with many cheerless birds upon bare twigs,

that piteously piped there for pain of the cold.

The hero on horseback hurries beneath them

through much marshland and mire, remaining alone,

fretting o'er his fate, lest he should fail

to see the service of that Sire that on that same night

of a girl was given—our guilt to destroy.

And therefore sighing he said: "I beseech Thee, Lord,

and Mary, who is mildest mother so dear,

of some harbor where highly I might hear mass

and Thy Matins tomorrow, meekly I ask,

and for this, priestly, I pray my 'Pater' and 'Ave'

And Creed."

He rode in his prayer

and cried for each misdeed.

He crossed himself with care

and said: "Christ's Cross me speed."

He'd not signed himself so but thrice

before seeing, through the sedge, a stronghold secure,

above a green, on high ground, garnished by boughs

of many thickset trunks attending the moat,

a castle the comeliest that ever a knight saw

perched on a plain, a park all about. (lns. 720–768)

Sir Gawain has found a human dwelling in which to celebrate Christmas. But his challenges are, it turns out, just beginning. Feel free to look up (or buy) the poem elsewhere to read the rest.

SCRIPTURE

Isaiah 59:15-21, Psalm 132, Luke 1

JOURNAL PROMPTS

What was the most meaningful Christmas Eve service or Mass you can remember? What aspects of God did it reveal to you?

Do you find it likelier that Jesus was born in a manger in a house, or a manger in a stable?
What would either version show us about Christ?

What's your favorite Christmas Eve memory?
What makes it so special?

CAROLS

"Angels We Have Heard on High"
"Let All Mortal Flesh Keep Silence"

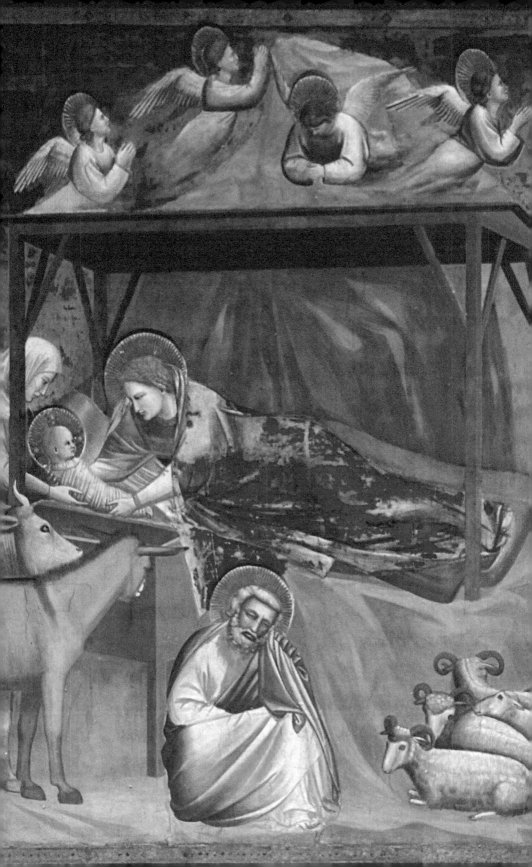

Christmas

O God, who makes us glad with the yearly remembrance of the birth of your only Son Jesus Christ: Grant that as we joyfully receive him for our Redeemer, so we may with sure confidence behold him when he shall come to be our Judge; who lives and reigns with you and the Holy Spirit, one God, world without end. Amen.

—*The Book of Common Prayer*

REFLECTION

Today we recognize the holy-yet-homely nature of the uncreated God who was born as a baby in a food trough, surrounded by his adopted people. Yesterday's reflection mentioned that in Christ, God—who defies our imagination and categories—became human. This means, we said, that as Jesus Christ, he entered into our human traditions, adopting them as well as reforming them. He sanctifies our feasts and fasts, and hallows them from within. At the same time, he prevents tradition from referring, emptily, to itself alone. The "meaning" of Christmas cannot be merely "Christmas," and if there is one weakness in Dickens's *A Christmas Carol* (and the thousands of Christmas specials that are its ill-formed offspring), it is that Christmas becomes self-referential, and therefore potentially idolatrous and meaningless. There have, of course, been many Christian sects that refuse to celebrate Christmas, from the Puritans to the Jehovah's Witnesses. Before dismissing these with a roll of the eye and wave of the hand, as modern-day Scrooges, we need to concede that they have a point. Christ came to redeem, but also to chasten, and one of his favorite subjects to criticize was tradition for its own sake. He pointed out that tradition can sometimes blind us to the very salvation it is supposed to lead us to, and it can even perpetuate injustice in the name of God.

And yet. Jesus drank and ate, and "desired greatly" to celebrate Passover with his friends and family. His first miracle turned water to wine at a wedding. He was labeled a glutton and a drunkard by those who hoped to save themselves through negation and asceticism. The celebrations in his honor, likewise, were often imperfect. Yet he did not refuse the riotous regal honors paid him by the crowd who welcomed him into Jerusalem with palm fronds (though they were insincere), or the children and fishermen who ran to him (though they were immature), or the anointing of the woman at Bethany (though she was disgraced). He received and delighted in every imperfect homage, perceiving within them that echo of the Father's eternal word to him: "This is my Son, whom I love; with him I am well pleased."

Yet if he is so honored by us, if he is so loved by the Father, if praise to him as King really is his due, then his judgment on our feasts and fasts, and still more of our selfishness and hypocrisy, is likewise his right and due. There is no joy in his homeliness without a recognition of, even a trembling before, his highness. We invite him into our homes at Christmas, yet he will not be domesticated. We often love the first coming of Christ—because it seems to make no demands on us—yet grow uncomfortable with the idea of his second coming, in full authority, to call us to account.

Nonetheless we must balance our affinity for the supposedly meek and mild baby in the manger with Yeats's line (if wrenched out of context): "A terrible beauty is born this day." Fearing judgment, we often prefer to keep this terrible beauty at a distance, refusing to risk our very selves, and thus we miss the greatest miracle of all: Our own birth into true life and true love. As John puts it: "Whoever confesses that Jesus is the Son of God, God abides in him, and he in God. So we have come to know and to believe the love that God has for us. God is love, and whoever abides in love abides in God, and God abides in him." It is in that place of communion with the Father and the Son that we hear the same echo, now addressed to us, calling us beloved children of God. He comes again, today and at the end of time, in judgment. But he also invites us to his Life, to his Feast, at Christmas and every day.

ACTIVITIES

Again, there are just about as many traditions for Christmas morning as there are families in the world. Do what you normally would do on Christmas and give a gift or two (probably your "biggest" gift) to the other people in your family or community who are celebrating Twelvetide with you. With our kids, we normally do stockings and give them whatever present their grandparents have bought for them, saving our own presents for subsequent days. If you do Santa, today might be a good day to give your kids whatever present Santa brought them as well. What we want to avoid is the sort of holiday glut of presents that leaves the rest of the day (and the rest of Christmas season!) feeling anticlimactic—as though Christmas is over or something. Really, Christmas has just begun. Here are a few ideas for the day, ranging from obvious to eccentric:

- Read Scripture, pray, and sing a carol before opening presents. Teach the carol to your kids (if applicable), or just learn it yourself.
- Go caroling at a nearby nursing home (obviously, this will take some arranging beforehand).
- Make a Christmas pie.
- Go on a cardinal hunt outside.
- Watch A Christmas Story on television like every other person in America.

- Create Christmas comics with friends or family members. Draw/write the first panel of a comic, then pass it to other people in your group to complete the next panel, as you complete the next panel in someone else's comic, and so on.
- For the past three years, we've watched *Tudor Monastery Farm at Christmas*, an impressive documentary showing how the twelve days of Christmas would have been celebrated around 1500.

GIFT GIVING

- One or two of your "biggest" gifts to the other people in your family or community who are celebrating Twelvetide with you.
- Stockings full of candy, small gifts, pieces of fruit, etc.
- NO CASH OPTION: Create a board game or card game for someone else and play it with them at some point during the day.

LITERATURE
A Christmas Carol

From Stave 3 of A Christmas Carol, *by Charles Dickens, the most famous work of literature to do with Christmas. In the scene below, Ebenezer Scrooge and the merry Ghost of Christmas Present are seeing how the first day of Christmas is celebrated by a number of different people in different stations of life. It is a fairly secular work, but I have chosen it for the way it weaves together merriment, concern for the downtrodden, and veneration of Christ. The excerpt here begins as the Ghost takes Scrooge to visit the house of his employee, Bob Cratchit.*

It was a remarkable quality of the Ghost (which Scrooge had observed at the baker's), that notwithstanding his gigantic size, he could accommodate himself to any place with ease; and that he stood beneath a low roof quite as gracefully and like a supernatural creature, as it was possible he could have done in any lofty hall.

And perhaps it was the pleasure the good Spirit had in showing off this power of his, or else it was his own kind, generous, hearty nature, and his sympathy with all poor men, that led him straight to Scrooge's clerk's; for there he went, and took Scrooge with him, holding to his robe; and on the threshold of the door the Spirit smiled, and stopped to bless Bob Cratchit's dwelling with the sprinkling of his torch. Think of that. Bob had but fifteen bob a-week himself; he pocketed on Saturdays but fifteen copies of his Christian name; and yet the Ghost of Christmas Present blessed his four-roomed house.

Then up rose Mrs Cratchit, Cratchit's wife, dressed out but poorly in a twice-turned gown, but brave in ribbons, which are cheap and make a goodly show for sixpence; and she laid the cloth, assisted by Belinda Cratchit, second of her daughters, also brave in ribbons; while Master Peter Cratchit plunged a fork into the saucepan of potatoes, and getting the corners of his monstrous shirt collar (Bob's private property, conferred upon his son and heir in honour of the day) into his mouth, rejoiced to find himself so gallantly attired, and yearned to show his linen in the fashionable Parks. And now two smaller Cratchits, boy and girl, came tearing in, screaming that outside the baker's they had smelt the goose, and known it for their own; and basking in luxurious thoughts of sage and onion, these young Cratchits danced about the table, and exalted Master Peter Cratchit to the skies, while he (not proud, although his collars nearly choked him) blew the fire, until the slow potatoes bubbling up, knocked loudly at the saucepan-lid to be let out and peeled.

"What has ever got your precious father then?" said Mrs Cratchit. "And your brother, Tiny Tim; And Martha warn't as late last Christmas Day by half-an-hour."

"Here's Martha, mother," said a girl, appearing as she spoke.

"Here's Martha, mother!" cried the two young Cratchits.

"Hurrah! There's such a goose, Martha!"

"Why, bless your heart alive, my dear, how late you are!" said Mrs

Cratchit, kissing her a dozen times, and taking off her shawl and bonnet for her with officious zeal.

"We'd a deal of work to finish up last night," replied the girl, "and had to clear away this morning, mother."

"Well. Never mind so long as you are come," said Mrs Cratchit. "Sit ye down before the fire, my dear, and have a warm, Lord bless ye."

"No, no. There's father coming," cried the two young Cratchits, who were everywhere at once. "Hide, Martha, hide!"

So Martha hid herself, and in came little Bob, the father, with at least three feet of comforter exclusive of the fringe, hanging down before him; and his threadbare clothes darned up and brushed, to look seasonable; and Tiny Tim upon his shoulder. Alas for Tiny Tim, he bore a little crutch, and had his limbs supported by an iron frame.

"Why, where's our Martha?" cried Bob Cratchit, looking round.

"Not coming," said Mrs Cratchit.

"Not coming!" said Bob, with a sudden declension in his high spirits; for he had been Tim's blood horse all the way from church, and had come home rampant. "Not coming upon Christmas Day?"

Martha didn't like to see him disappointed, if it were only in joke; so she came out prematurely from behind the closet door, and ran into his arms, while the two young Cratchits hustled Tiny Tim, and bore him off into the wash-house, that he might hear the pudding singing in the copper.

"And how did little Tim behave?" asked Mrs Cratchit, when she had rallied Bob on his credulity, and Bob had hugged his daughter to his heart's content.

"As good as gold," said Bob, "and better. Somehow he gets thoughtful sitting by himself so much, and thinks the strangest things you ever heard. He told me, coming home, that he hoped the people saw him in the church, because he was a cripple, and it might be pleasant to them to remember upon Christmas Day, who made lame beggars walk, and blind men see."

Bob's voice was tremulous when he told them this, and trembled more when he said that Tiny Tim was growing strong and hearty.

His active little crutch was heard upon the floor, and back came Tiny Tim before another word was spoken, escorted by his brother and sister to his stool before the fire; and while Bob, turning up his cuffs—as if, poor fellow, they were capable of being made more shabby—compounded some hot mixture in a jug with gin and lemons, and stirred it round and round and put it on the hob to simmer; Master Peter, and the two ubiquitous young Cratchits went to fetch the goose, with which they soon returned in high procession.

Such a bustle ensued that you might have thought a goose the rarest of all birds; a feathered phenomenon, to which a black swan was a matter of course—and in truth it was something very like it in that house. Mrs Cratchit made the gravy (ready beforehand in a little saucepan) hissing hot; Master Peter mashed the potatoes with incredible vigour; Miss Belinda sweetened up the apple-sauce; Martha dusted the hot plates; Bob took Tiny Tim beside him in a tiny corner at the table; the two young Cratchits set chairs for everybody, not forgetting themselves, and mounting guard upon their posts, crammed spoons into their mouths, lest they should shriek for goose before their turn came to be helped.

At last the dishes were set on, and grace was said. It was succeeded by a breathless pause, as Mrs Cratchit, looking slowly all along the carving-knife, prepared to plunge it in the breast; but when she did, and when the long expected gush of stuffing issued forth, one murmur of delight arose all round the board, and even Tiny Tim, excited by the two young Cratchits, beat on the table with the handle of his knife, and feebly cried Hurrah!

There never was such a goose. Bob said he didn't believe there ever was such a goose cooked. Its tenderness and flavour, size and cheapness, were the themes of universal admiration. Eked out by apple-sauce and mashed potatoes, it was a sufficient dinner for the whole family; indeed, as Mrs Cratchit said with great delight (surveying one small atom of a bone upon the dish), they hadn't ate it all at last. Yet every one had had enough, and the youngest Cratchits in particular, were steeped in sage and onion to the eyebrows. But now, the plates being changed by Miss Belinda, Mrs Cratchit left the room alone – too nervous to bear witnesses – to take the pudding up and bring it in.

Suppose it should not be done enough? Suppose it should break in turning out? Suppose somebody should have got over the wall of the back-yard, and stolen it, while they were merry with the goose – a supposition at which the two young Cratchits became livid? All sorts of horrors were supposed.

Hallo! A great deal of steam! The pudding was out of the copper. A smell like a washing-day. That was the cloth. A smell like an eating-house and a pastrycook's next door to each other, with a laundress's next door to that. That was the pudding. In half a minute Mrs Cratchit entered—flushed, but smiling proudly—with the pudding, like a speckled cannon-ball, so hard and firm, blazing in half of half-a-quartern of ignited brandy, and bedight with Christmas holly stuck into the top.

Oh, a wonderful pudding! Bob Cratchit said, and calmly too, that he regarded it as the greatest success achieved by Mrs Cratchit since their marriage. Mrs Cratchit said that now the weight was off her mind, she would confess she had had her doubts about the quantity of flour. Everybody had something to say about it, but nobody said or thought it was at all a small pudding for a large family. It would have been flat heresy to do so. Any Cratchit would have blushed to hint at such a thing.

At last the dinner was all done, the cloth was cleared, the hearth swept, and the fire made up. The compound in the jug being tasted, and considered perfect, apples and oranges were put upon the table, and a shovel-full of chestnuts on the fire. Then all the Cratchit family drew round the hearth, in what Bob Cratchit called a circle, meaning half a one; and at Bob Cratchit's elbow stood the family display of glass. Two tumblers, and a custard-cup without a handle.

These held the hot stuff from the jug, however, as well as golden goblets would have done; and Bob served it out with beaming looks, while the chestnuts on the fire sputtered and cracked noisily. Then Bob proposed:

"A Merry Christmas to us all, my dears. God bless us." Which all the family re-echoed.

"God bless us every one!" said Tiny Tim, the last of all.

He sat very close to his father's side upon his little stool. Bob held his withered little hand in his, as if he loved the child, and wished to keep him by his side, and dreaded that he might be taken from him.

"Spirit," said Scrooge, with an interest he had never felt before, "tell me if Tiny Tim will live."

"I see a vacant seat," replied the Ghost, "in the poor chimney-corner, and a crutch without an owner, carefully preserved. If these shadows remain unaltered by the Future, the child will die."

"No, no," said Scrooge. "Oh, no, kind Spirit. Say he will be spared."

"If these shadows remain unaltered by the Future, none other of my race," returned the Ghost, "will find him here. What then? If he be like to die, he had better do it, and decrease the surplus population."

Scrooge hung his head to hear his own words quoted by the Spirit, and was overcome with penitence and grief.

"Man," said the Ghost, "if man you be in heart, not adamant, forbear that wicked cant until you have discovered What the surplus is, and Where it is. Will you decide what men shall live, what men shall die? It may be, that in the sight of Heaven, you are more worthless and less fit to live than millions like this poor man's child. Oh God! To hear the Insect on the leaf pronouncing on the too much life among his hungry brothers in the dust."

Scrooge bent before the Ghost's rebuke, and trembling cast his eyes upon the ground. But he raised them speedily, on hearing his own name.

"Mr Scrooge!" said Bob; "I'll give you Mr Scrooge, the Founder of the Feast!"

"The Founder of the Feast indeed!" cried Mrs Cratchit, reddening. "I wish I had him here. I'd give him a piece of my mind to feast upon, and I hope he'd have a good appetite for it."

"My dear," said Bob, "the children. Christmas Day."

"It should be Christmas Day, I am sure," said she, "on which one drinks the health of such an odious, stingy, hard, unfeeling man as Mr Scrooge. You know he is, Robert. Nobody knows it better than you do, poor fellow."

"My dear," was Bob's mild answer, "Christmas Day."

"I'll drink his health for your sake and the Day's," said Mrs Cratchit, "not for his. Long life to him. A merry Christmas and a happy new year!—he'll be very merry and very happy, I have no doubt!"

The children drank the toast after her. It was the first of their proceedings which had no heartiness. Tiny Tim drank it last of all, but he didn't care twopence for it. Scrooge was the Ogre of the family. The mention of his name cast a dark shadow on the party, which was not dispelled for full five minutes.

After it had passed away, they were ten times merrier than before, from the mere relief of Scrooge the Baleful being done with. Bob Cratchit told them how he had a situation in his eye for Master Peter, which would bring in, if obtained, full five-and-sixpence weekly. The two young Cratchits laughed tremendously at the idea of Peter's being a man of business; and Peter himself looked thoughtfully at the fire from between his collars, as if he were deliberating what particular investments he should favour when he came into the receipt of that bewildering income. Martha, who was a poor apprentice at a milliner's, then told them what kind of work she had to do, and how many hours she worked at a stretch, and how she meant to lie abed to-morrow morning for a good long rest; to-morrow being a holiday she passed at home. Also how she had seen a countess and a lord some days before, and how the lord was much about as tall as Peter; at which Peter pulled up his collars so high that you couldn't have seen his head if you had been there. All this time the chestnuts and the jug went round and round; and by-and-bye they had a song, about a lost child travelling in the snow, from Tiny Tim, who had a plaintive little voice, and sang it very well indeed.

There was nothing of high mark in this. They were not a handsome family; they were not well dressed; their shoes were far from being water-proof; their clothes were scanty; and Peter might have known, and very likely did, the inside of a pawnbroker's. But, they were happy, grateful, pleased with one another, and contented with the time; and when they faded, and looked happier yet in the bright sprinklings of the Spirit's torch at parting, Scrooge had his eye upon them, and especially on Tiny Tim, until the last.

By this time it was getting dark, and snowing pretty heavily; and as Scrooge and the Spirit went along the streets, the brightness of the roaring fires in kitchens, parlours, and all sorts of rooms, was wonderful. Here, the flickering of the blaze showed preparations for a cosy dinner, with hot plates baking through and through before the fire, and deep red curtains, ready to be drawn to shut out cold and darkness. There all the children of the house were running out into the snow to meet their married sisters, brothers, cousins, uncles, aunts, and be the first to greet them. Here, again, were shadows on the window-blind of guests assembling; and there a group of handsome girls, all hooded and fur-booted, and all chattering at once, tripped lightly off to some near neighbour's house; where, woe upon the single man who saw them enter—artful witches, well they knew it—in a glow.

But, if you had judged from the numbers of people on their way to friendly gatherings, you might have thought that no one was at home to give them welcome when they got there, instead of every house expecting company, and piling up its fires half-chimney high.

Blessings on it, how the Ghost exulted. How it bared its breadth of breast, and opened its capacious palm, and floated on, outpouring, with a generous hand, its bright and harmless mirth on everything within its reach. The very lamplighter, who ran on before dotting the dusky street with specks of light, and who was dressed to spend the evening somewhere, laughed out loudly as the Spirit passed, though little kenned the lamplighter that he had any company but Christmas.

And now, without a word of warning from the Ghost, they stood upon a bleak and desert moor, where monstrous masses of rude stone were cast about, as though it were the burial-place of giants; and water spread itself wheresoever it listed—or would have done so, but for the frost that held it prisoner; and nothing grew but moss and furze, and coarse rank grass. Down in the west the setting sun had left a streak of fiery red, which glared upon the desolation for an instant, like a sullen eye, and frowning lower, lower, lower yet, was lost in the thick gloom of darkest night.

"What place is this?" asked Scrooge.

"A place where Miners live, who labour in the bowels of the earth," returned the Spirit.

"But they know me. See."

A light shone from the window of a hut, and swiftly they advanced towards it. Passing through the wall of mud and stone, they found a cheerful company assembled round a glowing fire. An old, old man and woman, with their children and their children's children, and another generation beyond that, all decked out gaily in their holiday attire. The old man, in a voice that seldom rose above the howling of the wind upon the barren waste, was singing them a Christmas song—it had been a very old song when he was a boy—and from time to time they all joined in the chorus. So surely as they raised their voices, the old man got quite blithe and loud; and so surely as they stopped, his vigour sank again.

The Spirit did not tarry here, but bade Scrooge hold his robe, and passing on above the moor, sped—whither. Not to sea? To sea. To Scrooge's horror, looking back, he saw the last of the land, a frightful range of rocks, behind them; and his ears were deafened by the thundering of water, as it rolled and roared, and raged among the dreadful caverns it had worn, and fiercely tried to undermine the earth.

Built upon a dismal reef of sunken rocks, some league or so from shore, on which the waters chafed and dashed, the wild year through, there stood a solitary lighthouse. Great heaps of sea-weed clung to its base, and storm-birds—born of the wind one might suppose, as sea-weed of the water—rose and fell about it, like the waves they skimmed. But even here, two men who watched the light had made a fire, that through the loophole in the thick stone wall shed out a ray of brightness on the awful sea. Joining their horny hands over the rough table at which they sat, they wished each other Merry Christmas in their can of grog; and one of them: the elder, too, with his face all damaged and scarred with hard weather, as the figure-head of an old ship might be: struck up a sturdy song that was like a Gale in itself.

Again the Ghost sped on, above the black and heaving sea – on, on – until, being far away, as he told Scrooge, from any shore, they lighted on a ship. They stood beside the helmsman at the wheel, the look-out in the bow, the officers who had the watch; dark, ghostly figures in their several stations; but every man among them hummed a Christmas tune, or had a Christmas thought, or spoke below his breath to his companion of some bygone Christmas Day, with homeward hopes belonging to it. And every man on board, waking or sleeping, good or bad, had had a kinder word for another on that day than on any day in the year; and had shared to some extent in its festivities; and had remembered those he cared for at a distance, and had known that they delighted to remember him.

It was a great surprise to Scrooge, while listening to the moaning of the wind, and thinking what a solemn thing it was to move on through the lonely darkness over an unknown abyss, whose depths were secrets as profound as Death: it was a great surprise to Scrooge, while thus engaged, to hear a hearty laugh. It was a much greater surprise to Scrooge to recognise it as his own nephew's and to find himself in a bright, dry, gleaming room, with the Spirit standing smiling by his side, and looking at that same nephew with approving affability.

"Ha, ha!" laughed Scrooge's nephew. "Ha, ha, ha!"

If you should happen, by any unlikely chance, to know a man more blest in a laugh than Scrooge's nephew, all I can say is, I should like to know him too. Introduce him to me, and I'll cultivate his acquaintance.

It is a fair, even-handed, noble adjustment of things, that while there is infection in disease and sorrow, there is nothing in the world so irresistibly contagious as laughter and good-humour. When Scrooge's nephew laughed in this way: holding his sides, rolling his head, and twisting his face into the most extravagant contortions: Scrooge's niece, by marriage, laughed as heartily as he. And their assembled friends being not a bit behindhand, roared out lustily.

"Ha, ha! Ha, ha, ha, ha!"

"He said that Christmas was a humbug, as I live!" cried Scrooge's nephew. "He believed it too." ... After tea they had some music. For they were a musical family, and knew what they were about, when they sung a Glee or Catch, I can assure you: especially Topper, who could growl away in the bass like a good one, and never swell the large veins in his forehead, or get red in the face over it. Scrooge's niece played well upon the harp; and played among other tunes a simple little air (a mere nothing: you might learn to whistle it in two minutes), which had been familiar to the child who fetched Scrooge from the boarding-school, as he had been reminded by the Ghost of Christmas Past. When this strain of music sounded, all the things that Ghost had shown him, came upon his mind; he softened more and more; and thought that if he could have listened to it often, years ago, he might have cultivated the kindnesses of life for his own happiness with his own hands, without resorting to the sexton's spade that buried Jacob Marley.

But they didn't devote the whole evening to music. After a while they played at forfeits; for it is good to be children sometimes, and never better than at Christmas, when its mighty Founder was a child himself.

SCRIPTURE

Genesis 2, Isaiah 11, Luke 1, Psalm 2 , 1 John 4:7-16

JOURNAL PROMPTS

Describe two very different Christmases you've experienced.
What made each of them meaningful?

Which of the Christmas celebrations described in *A Christmas
Carol* most resembles your own?

What are some of the ways you'd most like to celebrate the
Incarnation this Christmas season?
Feel free to look ahead in this book for ideas.

Meditate on how Christ changes our feasts. In what ways has being
a Christian changed the way you celebrate events?

CAROLS

"Hark! The Herald Angels Sing"
"The Wexford Carol"

The Second Day

The Feast of St. Stephen

We give you thanks, O Lord of glory, for the example of the first martyr Stephen, who looked up to heaven and prayed for his persecutors to your Son Jesus Christ, who stands at your right hand; where he lives and reigns with you and the Holy Spirit, one God, in glory everlasting. Amen.

—*The Book of Common Prayer*

REFLECTION

It's probably best to say this now—most of the traditional feast days celebrated by the Church commemorate martyrdoms, and there will consequently be a lot of reflection on martyrs in this book. This line-up seems a bit like a trick at first: "Sure, get us to celebrate Christmas with a nice cover image of a new baby and a bunch of astrologers and animals—only to fill the inside of the book with images of people dying in grotesque ways. Then we will all feel guilty for being happy and having fun during this season, which forces us to ask God to forgive us for our laughter. Well, the jig is up! Do you really expect us to party one minute and soberly listen to stories of martyrs (ancient and modern) the next?"

Well, I don't. I don't, at any rate, expect anyone (myself included) to do it *perfectly*. But I think it's probably worth attempting, because traditionally these are Feast Days, not Fast Days. The day of a saint's death is his "dies natalis," his "birthday," when (originally) even the close relatives and friends of this or that martyr would commemorate him or her by having little picnics around his or her grave. We should not allow the fact of suffering in the world—past or present—to guilt us into joylessness and ingratitude for the gifts we have been given in the here-and-now. But we should allow the memory of the martyrs, from Stephen to those currently losing their lives daily, to anchor our joy and prevent it from drifting into flippancy. There is, of course, a point at which laughter and gaiety may become joyless and drab, having everything to do with cynicism and nothing whatever to do with a full and happy life. Remembrance of death—Christ's, those of the martyrs, our own—does not rob us of the joy of Christmas any more than it robs us of the joy of life. Instead, such remembrance redeems games, gift-giving, food, drink—and I do not think that the saints, in their current bliss, envy us these things. Rather they died, in part, to give others eternal joy that cannot help but spill over into temporal happiness. Even those currently persecuted, who have not yet lost their lives, cannot begrudge others the comforts they may no longer share. But they do ask that we remember them to each other and to the Lord. Too often, we take the opposite tack, believing that our frequent tight-fistedness is somehow ameliorated by the fact that we don't enjoy our riches!

It's a fictional carol, but we probably wouldn't be wrong to take a page from the book of "Good King Wenceslas," who honored the memory of St. Stephen not by stoicism and grim fasting but by sharing his food and wine with the poorest in his kingdom:

> "Bring me food and bring me wine, bring me pine logs hither,
> You and I will see him dine, when we bear them thither."

It is an appropriate song to sing at Christmastide because Wenceslas's act echoes the extravagant generosity of God, who in an overflow of joy gave us his very self in birth and death, that we might all share his human-yet-eternal life. This feast in the martyr's memory is not a refusal of joy, but a deepening of it, as darkness makes Christmas lights brighter and the cold enriches fire. But I don't say this to end with some sort of cliché, like "It's only because of death that life is beautiful in the first place," or some nonsense of that sort. There are real, horrible trag-edies going on all the time, and we have yet to understand how they will be redeemed. But we should not use this as an excuse to refuse God's gifts to us. We must, further, acknowledge that in some way, Christ's birth into the world, his death, and his resurrection were the beginning of a great miracle in which our constant and bewildering defeats may become victories, and in which our deaths, too, open the way to greater life, both in this world and the next. Death will be swallowed up in victory, and the day of our birth will dawn. Until then, we mourn and celebrate in hope and joy.

ACTIVITIES

Celebrate "Boxing Day": Wrap a present (or cash) in a box, and give it to a person who performs a (normally unthanked) civil service, such as a mail carrier or a garbage collector (you may, of course, have to wrap the gift today and give it to them when you next see them—and they may not be allowed to accept gifts). This old British tradition can be construed along broader lines, however: think about creative ways to show your appreciation for those whose work often goes unthanked. This could be as simple as leaving a larger tip than usual for a server.

- Visit friends and family throughout the day, eating, drinking, talking, and giving gifts. Feel free to travel in a group and perform plays and songs for them, as is traditional in parts of Ireland.
- Ride in a sleigh pulled by a horse, as was traditional in Finland. Failing that, take a ride in a horse-drawn carriage, or, if the weather is amenable, go sledding or skiing.
- Read one of the books of Moses in memory of St. Stephen, and compare with his summary of Israel's history in Acts.
- Take a cue from King Wenceslas and find a creative way to serve the homeless, whether by volunteering at a soup kitchen or something else.

- Read about present-day martyred Christians around the world, and thank God for their witness. Then, pray for the persecuted Church: *Aid to the Church in Need, Persecution.org,* and *The Voice of the Martyrs* are all good resources for this. There is also a *Voice of the Martyrs* app to help you stand in solidarity with the persecuted Church. Globally, about one in twelve Christians is severely persecuted, but this fact is often ignored by both Christians and non-Christians in the West. Some of the most ancient communities of Christians—those in Iraq and Syria—have been wiped out almost completely in the past half-decade. Persecution is ramping up in other countries as well, such as India, where rising nationalism has brought about the persecution of many Christians. It may be a good idea to write your senator or congressperson about these issues as well and, most of all, to pray for the global Church and their persecutors.

GIFT GIVING

- Give just one of the gifts you did not give on Christmas Day.
- Make a donation in someone's name to an organization such as *The Voice of the Martyrs* that supports persecuted Christians or to another group raising awareness of persecuted religious minorities in other countries.
- NO CASH OPTION: Bake Christmas cookies for other people in the shape of turtledoves. Give each person two of them. Or give postal workers, Amazon drivers, etc., a box of baked goods!

LITERATURE
The Wind in the Willows

In this classic children's story by Kenneth Grahame (1908), Mole and Rat, best friends, have just returned to Mole's underground house in the dead of winter, after about a year of adventuring. They are cleaning up and eating what meager provisions Mole has left, when they are visited by some caroling field-mice.

Encouraged by his inspiriting companion, the Mole roused himself and dusted and polished with energy and heartiness, while the Rat, running to and fro with armfuls of fuel, soon had a cheerful blaze roaring up the chimney. He hailed the Mole to come and warm himself; but Mole promptly had another fit of the blues, dropping down on a couch in dark despair and burying his face in his duster. "Rat," he moaned, "how about your supper, you poor, cold, hungry, weary animal? I've nothing to give you—nothing—not a crumb!"

"What a fellow you are for giving in!" said the Rat reproachfully. "Why, only just now I saw a sardine-opener on the kitchen dresser, quite distinctly; and everybody knows that means there are sardines about somewhere in the neighbourhood. Rouse yourself! pull yourself together, and come with me and forage."

They went and foraged accordingly, hunting through every cupboard and turning out every drawer. The result was not so very depressing after all, though of course it might have been better; a tin of sardines—a box of captain's biscuits, nearly full—and a German sausage encased in silver paper.

"There's a banquet for you!" observed the Rat, as he arranged the table. "I know some animals who would give their ears to be sitting down to supper with us to-night!"

"No bread!" groaned the Mole dolorously; "no butter, no——"

"No pate de foie gras, no champagne!" continued the Rat, grinning. "And that reminds me—what's that little door at the end of the passage? Your cellar, of course! Every luxury in this house! Just you wait a minute."

He made for the cellar-door, and presently reappeared, somewhat dusty, with a bottle of beer in each paw and another under each arm, "Self-indulgent beggar you seem to be, Mole," he observed. "Deny yourself nothing. This is really the jolliest little place I ever was in. Now, wherever did you pick up those prints? Make the place look so home-like, they do. No wonder you're so fond of it, Mole. Tell us all about it, and how you came to make it what it is."

Then, while the Rat busied himself fetching plates, and knives and forks, and mustard which he mixed in an egg-cup, the Mole, his bosom still heaving with the stress of his recent emotion, related—somewhat shyly at first, but with more freedom as he warmed to his subject—how this was planned, and how that was thought out, and how this was got through a windfall from an aunt, and that was a wonderful find and a bargain, and this other thing was bought out of laborious savings and a certain amount of "going without." His spirits finally quite restored, he must needs go and caress his possessions, and take a lamp and show off their points to his visitor and expatiate on them, quite forgetful of the supper they both so much needed; Rat, who was desperately hungry but strove to conceal it, nodding seriously, examining with a puckered brow, and saying, "wonderful," and "most remarkable," at intervals, when the chance for an observation was given him.

At last the Rat succeeded in decoying him to the table, and had just got seriously to work with the sardine-opener when sounds were heard from the fore-court without—sounds like the scuffling of small feet in the gravel and a confused murmur of tiny voices, while broken sentences reached them— "Now, all in a line—hold the lantern up a bit, Tommy— clear your throats first—no coughing after I say one, two, three.—Where's young Bill?—Here, come on, do, we're all a-waiting—"

"What's up?" inquired the Rat, pausing in his labours.

"I think it must be the field-mice," replied the Mole, with a touch of pride in his manner. "They go round carol-singing regularly at this time of the year. They're quite an institution in these parts. And they never pass me over—they come to Mole End last of all; and I used to give them hot drinks, and supper too sometimes, when I could afford it. It will be like old times to hear them again."

"Let's have a look at them!" cried the Rat, jumping up and running to the door.

It was a pretty sight, and a seasonable one, that met their eyes when they flung the door open. In the fore-court, lit by the dim rays of a horn lantern, some eight or ten little fieldmice stood in a semicircle, red worsted comforters round their throats, their fore-paws thrust deep into their pockets, their feet jigging for warmth. With bright beady eyes they glanced shyly at each other, sniggering a little, sniffing and applying coat-sleeves a good deal. As the door opened, one of the elder ones that carried the lantern was just saying, "Now then, one, two, three!" and forthwith their shrill little voices uprose on the air, singing one of the old-time carols that their forefathers composed in fields that were fallow and held by frost, or when snow-bound in chimney corners, and handed down to be sung in the miry street to lamp-lit windows at Yule-time.

CAROL
Villagers all, this frosty tide,
Let your doors swing open wide,
Though wind may follow, and snow beside,
   Yet draw us in by your fire to bide;

Joy shall be yours in the morning!

Here we stand in the cold and the sleet,
Blowing fingers and stamping feet,
Come from far away you to greet—
You by the fire and we in the street—
Bidding you joy in the morning!

For ere one half of the night was gone,
Sudden a star has led us on,
Raining bliss and benison—
Bliss to-morrow and more anon,
Joy for every morning!

Goodman Joseph toiled through the snow—
Saw the star o'er a stable low;
Mary she might not further go—
Welcome thatch, and litter below!
Joy was hers in the morning!

And then they heard the angels tell
"Who were the first to cry NOWELL?
Animals all, as it befell,
In the stable where they did dwell!
Joy shall be theirs in the morning!"

The voices ceased, the singers, bashful but smiling, exchanged sidelong glances, and silence succeeded—but for a moment only. Then, from up above and far away, down the tunnel they had so lately travelled was borne to their ears in a faint musical hum the sound of distant bells ringing a joyful and clangorous peal.

"Very well sung, boys!" cried the Rat heartily. "And now come along in, all of you, and warm yourselves by the fire, and have something hot!"

"Yes, come along, field-mice," cried the Mole eagerly. "This is quite like old times! Shut the door after you. Pull up that settle to the fire. Now, you just wait a minute, while we—O, Ratty!" he cried in despair, plumping down on a seat, with tears impending. "Whatever are we doing? We've nothing to give them!"

"You leave all that to me," said the masterful Rat. "Here, you with the lantern! Come over this way. I want to talk to you. Now, tell me, are there any shops open at this hour of the night?"

"Why, certainly, sir," replied the field-mouse respectfully. "At this time of the year our shops keep open to all sorts of hours."

"Then look here!" said the Rat. "You go off at once, you and your lantern, and you get me—"

Here much muttered conversation ensued, and the Mole only heard bits of it, such as "—Fresh, mind!—no, a pound of that will do—see you get Buggins's, for I won't have any other—no, only the best—if you can't get it there, try somewhere else—yes, of course, home-made, no tinned stuff—well then, do the best you can!" Finally, there was a chink of coin passing from paw to paw, the field-mouse was provided with an ample basket for his purchases, and off he hurried, he and his lantern.

The rest of the field-mice, perched in a row on the settle, their small legs swinging, gave themselves up to enjoyment of the fire, and toasted their chilblains till they tingled; while the Mole, failing to draw them into easy conversation, plunged into family history and made each of them recite the names of his numerous brothers, who were too young, it appeared, to be allowed to go out a-carolling this year, but looked forward very shortly to winning the parental consent.

The Rat, meanwhile, was busy examining the label on one of the beer-bottles. "I perceive this to be Old Burton," he remarked approvingly. "SENSIBLE Mole! The very thing! Now we shall be able to mull some ale! Get the things ready, Mole, while I draw the corks." It did not take long to prepare the brew and thrust the tin heater well into the red heart of the fire; and soon every field-mouse was sipping and coughing and choking (for a little mulled ale goes a long way) and wiping his eyes and laughing and forgetting he had ever been cold in all his life.

"They act plays too, these fellows," the Mole explained to the Rat. "Make them up all by themselves, and act them afterwards. And very well they do it, too! They gave us a capital one last year, about a field-mouse who was captured at sea by a Barbary corsair, and made to row in a galley; and when he escaped and got home again, his lady-love had gone into a convent. Here, YOU! You were in it, I remember. Get up and recite a bit." The field-mouse addressed got up on his legs, giggled shyly, looked round the room, and remained absolutely tongue-tied. His comrades cheered him on, Mole coaxed and encouraged him, and the Rat went so far as to take him by the shoulders and shake him; but nothing could overcome his stage-fright. They were all busily engaged on him like watermen applying the Royal Humane Society's regulations to a case of long submersion, when the latch clicked, the door opened, and the field-mouse with the lantern reappeared, staggering under the weight of his basket.

There was no more talk of play-acting once the very real and solid contents of the basket had been tumbled out on the table. Under the generalship of Rat, everybody was set to do something or to fetch something. In a very few minutes supper was ready, and Mole, as he took the head of the table in a sort of a dream, saw a lately barren board set thick with savoury comforts; saw his little friends' faces brighten and beam as they fell to without delay; and then let himself loose—for he was famished indeed—on the provender so magically provided, thinking what a happy home-coming this had turned out, after all. As they ate, they talked of old times, and the field-mice gave him the local gossip up to date, and answered as well as they could the hundred questions he had to ask them. The Rat said little or nothing, only taking care that each guest had what he wanted, and plenty of it, and that Mole had no trouble or anxiety about anything.

They clattered off at last, very grateful and showering wishes of the season, with their jacket pockets stuffed with remembrances for the small brothers and sisters at home. When the door had closed on the last of them and the chink of the lanterns had died away, Mole and Rat kicked the fire up, drew their chairs in, brewed themselves a last nightcap of mulled ale, and discussed the events of the long day. At last the Rat, with a tremendous yawn, said, "Mole, old chap, I'm ready to drop. Sleepy is simply not the word. That your own bunk over on that side? Very well, then, I'll take this. What a ripping little house this is! Everything so handy!"

He clambered into his bunk and rolled himself well up in the blankets, and slumber gathered him forthwith, as a swathe of barley is folded into the arms of the reaping machine.

The weary Mole also was glad to turn in without delay, and soon had his head on his pillow, in great joy and contentment. But ere he closed his eyes he let them wander round his old room, mellow in the glow of the firelight that played or rested on familiar and friendly things which had long been unconsciously a part of him, and now smilingly received him back, without rancour. He was now in just the frame of mind that the tactful Rat had quietly worked to bring about in him. He saw clearly how plain and simple—how narrow, even—it all was; but clearly, too, how much it all meant to him, and the special value of some such anchorage in one's existence. He did not at all want to abandon the new life and its splendid spaces, to turn his back on sun and air and all they offered him and creep home and stay there; the upper world was all too strong, it called to him still, even down there, and he knew he must return to the larger stage. But it was good to think he had this to come back to; this place which was all his own, these things which were so glad to see him again and could always be counted upon for the same simple welcome.

SCRIPTURE

Genesis 3, Isaiah 53, Acts 6:8-7:6; 7:44-7:60,
Matthew 21:33-46

JOURNAL PROMPTS

What were some of God's gifts to you this past year?
Try to name at least twelve, and thank God for them.

How can you help those who are overlooked know they are appreciated by you and by God today? Think of the poor (as Wenceslas does), the persecuted, and those in service industries.
Can you think of creative ways to bless them?

What do you think today's literary passage from *The Wind in the Willows* shows us about the character of God, as well as the Incarnation?

CAROLS

"Good King Wenceslas"
"O Come All Ye Faithful"

The Third Day

The Feast of John the Apostle & Evangelist

Shed upon your Church, O Lord, the brightness of your light, that we, being illumined by the teaching of your apostle and evangelist John, may so walk in the light of your truth, that at length we may attain to the fullness of eternal life; through Jesus Christ our Lord, who lives and reigns with you and the Holy Spirit, one God, for ever and ever. Amen.

—The Book of Common Prayer

REFLECTION

Of all the gospel writers, John seems to have the greatest capacity for abstraction. Mark's is the earliest account, fired throughout with action and immediacy. He seems content to begin with Jesus' adult ministry, skipping his birth and other such preludes. Luke the physician is the careful reporter and biographer, and it is from him that we get both the most popular story of Jesus' birth as well as that of John the Baptist. Matthew is obsessed with Jesus' earthly mission to fulfill the Scriptures and gives us the story of the Magi, Herod, and the slaughter of the Innocents—the implication being that Jesus is the new Moses, saved from a new kind of Pharaoh.

Rather than begin with Jesus' ministry on earth, though, or with Jesus' birth as a human, John begins his gospel in Heaven: "In the beginning was the Word, and the Word was with God, and the Word was God." It is the most idiosyncratic, literary, and mystical of the four gospels. It is replete with meaning—with interpretation (often given by Christ, "the Word" himself) of every little event or miracle—and yet the interpretations themselves can sound like new riddles: "What does this have to do with me? My hour has not yet come"; "You must be born again"; "I and the Father are one." The stories are arranged in such a way as to be almost sermon illustrations for the teaching of this Word.

You would think that someone as mystical and abstract as John would not have much of an eye for narrative detail, but again and again, we get fascinating little descriptions that we don't have in the other gospels: the master of the wedding feast commenting on the custom of serving inferior wine to drunk people; Jesus' cure of the blind man by spitting on dirt to make mud; the phrase "Jesus wept"; the towel he girt around his waist; John himself leaning on Jesus' breast; the folded face-cloth in the tomb; the risen Christ eating a fish. Here is a God breaking out of skies and temples to walk with people, imbuing everyday life with the sacred, or perhaps reminding us of its spiritual nature even as he redeems it.

John likewise reminds us again and again that "the Word became flesh and dwelt among us"; he had (and has) a thoroughly human life. And yet the humility of Jesus is not, in the end, the point. He is humble— more humble, certainly, than his followers—but his very lowness serves to manifest his glory among fallen humans: "We have seen his glory, the glory as of the only Son from the Father, full of grace and truth." John says that Christ brings light into darkness. His humanity does not lower Godhood but instead raises us to a place where true worship ("in spirit and in truth") is actually possible: "I am ascending to my Father and your Father, to my God and your God." There is a breathtaking, uncomfortable familiarity here, not only between John and Jesus, but between God and his worshipers. We become something closer than family to the Trinity itself, because we now share Christ's place vis-à-vis the Father. Because he is our kin, we lean on his breast, with John, and receive the Holy Spirit with his breath.

We struggle with this. We usually want a God who is not quite so near. And that is why we have John's writings. They remind us of who we are, of how we are to think of ourselves, and of how we are to treat each other. Christ gives John his own relationship with the Father, and John extends that same relationship to us. Yet each time this relationship is extended, it is enriched, so that it encompasses another human soul. Thus John reminds us: "God is love"; "Beloved, let us love one another. For love is of God, and everyone who loves has been born of God and knows God"; "Love one another as I have loved you. So [in this way] you must love one another. By this all men will know that you are my disciples, if you love one another"; "Simon, Son of Jonah, do you truly love me more than these? Then feed my lambs" ; "For God so [in this way] loved the world, that he gave his only begotten Son, that whoever believes in him should not perish but have everlasting life."

The point of John's gospel—of his life, for that matter—is Christ, not John. This much is clear from the fact that the evangelist does not even name himself throughout the entirety of the book, referring to himself instead as "the disciple whom Jesus loved," or just "the disciple." Despite this, John's is the most distinctive of the four gospels, the most marked with his own personality. It is as though the principle of mutual glorification that exists within the Trinity ("glorify your Son that the Son may glorify you") has been extended through John's friend Jesus to John himself. And indeed it has. We can enjoy John's glory during this day, for it is ultimately God's glory, Father, Son, and Holy Ghost.

ACTIVITIES

In keeping with the Christmas and Johannine theme of light against darkness, spend some time outside (weather permitting) studying the stars. Try to identify particular constellations.

- If your tradition permits, have some mulled wine (or another warm, festive drink, if not) in memory of the Wedding at Cana.
- Enjoy a firepit outside (brrr!) or light a log in your fireplace and enjoy the warmth while sitting together.

- Read the three epistles of John together (the latter two books are quite short) and talk about what it might look like to put John's advice into practice in your everyday life.
- See the "No cash option" under "gift giving" for today.
- Spend time creatively meditating on one of the chapters in John's gospel. Read it over and over or illustrate it or set it to music.

GIFT GIVING

- Give someone a candle, a flashlight, or another luminous present and read the opening of John's gospel with the other lights turned off.
- NO CASH OPTION: Sit down with your family or community as you write down the things you appreciate about one another. Then, take turns reading your notes to each other out loud. Put the notes in an envelope with the date on it so that they can look at and be encouraged throughout the coming year by the things you've said.

LITERATURE
Grettir's Saga: Glam's Ghost

For some reason, Christmas is a good time for ghost stories. Here is one from a thirteenth/fourteenth century Icelandic saga called Grettir's Saga *(Grettissaga), translated around 1900 by William Morris and Eirikr Magnusson. The celebration of Yule predated Christmas in Northern Europe, but this is an example of what can happen to you if you're a surly shepherd who refuses to keep the newfangled Advent fast preceding the Christmas feasts (spoiler: you become a revenant who rides roofs and kills everything). This excerpt opens as a man named Thorhall is trying to find a new shepherd who is not spooked by the ghost already haunting his settlement.*

(A quick note on the text: I am using it here because it is out of copyright, but Morris really loves to use archaic words in his translations. It's pretty readable though, even if you encounter some words you're not used to.)

Soon they met together, and Thorhall asked him of his name. He said that he was called Glam. This man was great of growth, uncouth to look on; his eyes were grey and glaring, and his hair was wolf-grey.

Thorhall stared at him somewhat when he saw this man, till he saw that this was he to whom he had been sent.

"What work hast thou best will to do?" said Thorhall.

Glam said, "That he was of good mind to watch sheep in winter."

"Wilt thou watch my sheep?" said Thorhall. "Skapti has given thee to my will."

"So only shall my service avail thee, if I go of my own will, for I am evil of mood if matters mislike me," quoth Glam.

"I fear no hurt thereof," said Thorhall, "and I will that thou fare to my house."

"That may I do," said Glam, "perchance there are some troubles there?"

"Folk deem the place haunted," said Thorhall.

"Such bugs will not scare me," quoth Glam; "life seems to me less irksome thereby."

"It must needs seem so," said Thorhall, "and truly it is better that a mannikin be not there."

Thereafter they struck bargain together, and Glam is to come at winter nights: then they parted, and Thorhall found his horses even where he had just been searching. Thorhall rode home, and thanked Skapti for his good deed.

Summer slipped away, and Thorhall heard nought of his shepherd, nor did any man know aught about him; but at the appointed time he came to Thorhall-stead. The bonder greeted him well, but none of the other folk could abide him, and the good wife least of all.

Now he took to the sheep-watching, and little trouble it seemed to give him; he was big-voiced and husky, and all the beasts would run together when he whooped. There was a church at Thorhall-stead, but nowise would Glam come therein; he was a loather of church-song, and godless, foul-tempered, and surly, and no man might abide him.

Now passed the time till it came to Yule-eve; then Glam got up and straightway called for his meat. The good wife said, "No Christian man is wont to eat meat this day, be-cause that on the morrow is the first day of Yule," says she, "wherefore must men first fast to-day."

He answers, "Many follies have ye, whereof I see no good come, nor know I that men fare better now than when they paid no heed to such things; and methinks the ways of men were better when they were called heathens; and now will I have my meat, and none of this fooling."

Then said the housewife, "I know for sure that thou shall fare ill to-day, if thou takest up this evil turn."

Glam bade her bring food straightway, and said that she should fare the worse else. She durst do but as he would, and so when he was full, he went out, growling and grumbling.

Now the weather was such, that mirk was over all, and the snow-flakes drave down, and great din there was, and still all grew much the worse, as the day slipped away.

Men heard the shepherd through the early morning, but less of him as the day wore; then it took to snowing, and by evening there was a great storm; then men went to church, and thus time drew on to nightfall; and Glam came not home; then folk held talk, as to whether search should not be made for him, but, because of the snow-storm and pitch darkness, that came to nought.

Now he came not home on the night of Yule-eve; and thus men abide till after the time of worship; but further on in the day men fared out to the search, and found the sheep scattered wide about in fens, beaten down by the storm, or strayed up into the mountains. Thereafter they came on a great beaten place high up in the valley, and they thought it was as if strong wrestling had gone on there; for that all about the stones had been uptorn and the earth withal; now they looked closely and saw where Glam lay a little way therefrom; he was dead, and as blue as hell, and as great as a neat.

Huge loathing took them, at the sight of him, and they shuddered in their souls at him, yet they strove to bring him to church, but could get him only as far as a certain gil-edge a little way below.

Then they fared home to the farm, and told the bonder what had happed. He asked what was like to have been Glam's bane. They said they had tracked steps as great as if a cask-bottom had been stamped down, from there where the beaten place was, up to beneath sheer rocks which were high up the valley, and there along went great stains of blood. Now men drew from this, that the evil wight which had been there before had killed Glam, but had got such wounds as had been full enough for him, for of him none has since been ware.

The second day of Yule, men went afresh to try to bring Glam to church; drag horses were put to him, but could move him nowhere where they had to go on even ground and not down hill; then folk had to go away therefrom leaving things done so far. The third day the priest fared with them, and they sought all day, but found not Glam. The priest would go no more on such search, but the herdsman was found whenso the priest was not in their company. Then they let alone striving to bring him to church, and buried him there whereto he had been brought.

A little time after men were ware that Glam lay not quiet. Folk got great hurt therefrom, so that many fell into swoons when they saw him, but others lost their wits thereby. But just after Yule men thought they saw him home at the farm. Folk became exceeding afeard thereat, and many fled there and then. Next Glam took to riding the house-roofs at night, so that he went nigh to breaking them in. Now he walked well-nigh night and day. Hardly durst men fare up into the dale, though they had errands enough there. And much scathe the men of the country-side deemed all this.

In the spring Thorhall got serving-men, and set up house at his farm; then the hauntings began to go off while the sun was at its height; and so things went on to midsummer. That summer a ship came out to Hunawater, wherein was a man named Thorgaut. He was an outlander of kin, big and stout, and two men's strength he had. He was unhired and single, and would fain do some work, for he was moneyless. Now Thorhall rode to the ship, and asked Thorgaut if he would work for him. Thorgaut said that might be, and moreover that he was not nice about work.

"Be sure in thy mind," said Thorhall, "that mannikins are of small avail there because of the hauntings that have been going on there for one while now; for I will not draw thee on by wiles."

Thorgaut answers, "I deem not myself given up, though I should see some wraithlings; matters will not be light when I am scared, nor will I give up my service for that."

Now they come speedily to a bargain, and Thorgaut is to watch the sheep when winter comes. So the summer wore on, and Thorgaut betook himself to the shepherding at winter nights, and all liked him well. But ever came Glam home and rode the house-roofs; this Thorgaut deemed sport enough, and quoth he,

"The thrall must come nigher to scare me."

Thorhall bade him keep silence over that. "Better will it be that ye have no trial together."

Thorgaut said, "Surely all might is shaken out of you, nor shall I drop down betwixt morn and eve at such talk."

Now so things go through the winter till Yule-tide. On Yule eve the shepherd would fare out to his sheep. Then said the good wife, "Need is it that things go not the old way."

He answered, "Have no fear thereof, goodwife; something worth telling of will betide if I come not back."

And thereafter he went to his sheep; and the weather was somewhat cold, and there was much snow. Thorgaut was wont to come home when twilight had set in, and now he came not at that time. Folk went to church as they were wont. Men now thought things looked not unlike what they did before; the bonder would have search made for the shepherd, but the church-goers begged off, and said that they would not give themselves into the hands of trolls by night; so the bonder durst not go, and the search came to nought.

Yule-day, when men were full, they fared out and searched for the shepherd; they first went to Glam's cairn, because men thought that from his deeds came the loss of the herdsman. But when they came nigh to the cairn, there they saw great tidings, for there they found the shepherd, and his neck was broken, and every bone in him smashed. Then they brought him to church, and no harm came to men from Thorgaut afterwards.

But Glam began afresh to wax mighty; and such deeds he wrought, that all men fled away from Thorhall-stead, except the good man and his goodwife. Now the same neatherd had long been there, and Thorhall would not let him go, because of his good will and safe ward; he was well on in years, and was very loth to fare away, for he saw that all things the bonder had went to nought from not being watched.

Now after midwinter one morning the housewife fared to the byre to milk the cows after the wonted time; by then was it broad daylight, for none other than the neatherd would trust themselves out before day; but he went out at dawn. She heard great cracking in the byre, with bellowing and roaring; she ran back crying out, and said she knew not what uncouth things were going on in the byre.

The bonder went out and came to the cows, which were goring one another; so he thought it not good to go in there, but went in to the hay-barn. There he saw where lay the neatherd, and had his head in one boose and his feet in the other; and he lay cast on his back. The bonder went up to him, and felt him all over with his hand, and finds soon that he was dead, and the spine of him broken asunder; it had been broken over the raised stone-edge of a boose.

Now the goodman thought there was no abiding there longer; so he fled away from the farm with all that he might take away; but all such live stock as was left behind Glam killed, and then he fared all over the valley and destroyed farms up from Tongue. But Thorhall was with his friends the rest of the winter.

No man might fare up the dale with horse or hound, because straightway it was slain. But when spring came, and the sun-light was the greatest, somewhat the hauntings abated; and now would Thorhall go back to his own land; he had no easy task in getting servants, nathless he set up house again at Thorhall-stead; but all went the same way as before; for when autumn came, the hauntings began to wax again; the bonder's daughter was most set on, and fared so that she died thereof. Many redes were sought, but nought could be done; men thought it like that all Waterdale would be laid waste if nought were found to better this. What will happen to the good people and cattle at Thorhall-stead?

Will a hero (surly or otherwise) come to put an end to the depredations of Glam? What in the world is a bonder? Find out the answer to most of these questions by reading the rest of the story, starting in Chapter 34.

GRETTIR OVERTHROWS THORIR REDBEARD

SCRIPTURE

Micah 7, John 1:1-18, 1 John 4

JOURNAL PROMPTS

In what way does John's glory extend God's glory, rather than rivaling it? To what extent is the glory of the saints (or any good things) in competition with God's glory, and to what extent do these glories further enhance the glory of God?

What does it mean that we share Christ's relationship with the Father?

Read the segment from Grettir's Saga for today. What do you make of the common practice of telling ghost stories at Christmas? Is it pagan superstition? Harmless fun? Symbolic and meaningful in some way? How do you account for the ghosts in the Bible?

CAROLS

"The Boar's Head Carol"
"God Rest Ye Merry Gentlemen"

The Fourth Day

The Feast of the Holy Innocents

We remember today, O God, the slaughter of the holy innocents of Bethlehem by King Herod. Receive, we pray, into the arms of your mercy all innocent victims; and by your great might frustrate the designs of the evil tyrants and establish your rule of justice, love, and peace; through Jesus Christ our Lord, who lives and reigns with you, in the unity of the Holy Spirit, one God, for ever and ever. Amen.

—The Book of Common Prayer

REFLECTION

If celebrating twelve days of Christmas doesn't seem counter-cultural enough to you, then celebrating the remembrance of King Herod's massacre of the innocents will firmly place you against the grain. Congratulations...you're crazy! Just kidding. Sort of.

If the readings didn't make it clear, this feast day celebrates when King Herod decided to massacre all the baby boys, thinking that he could somehow kill the Christ child in one fell swoop. He kills many young boys (aged 2 and under) but he never finds Jesus (because Jesus' family departed from Bethlehem). Jesus' family only returns home once they learn of Herod's death.

This story of the massacre of the innocents casts a somber mood in the midst of a joyous season. So why on earth would we celebrate this day?

There are several ways you could view this feast.

One take would be to make a silly tradition that would involve hitting kids with sticks. The English did this for Childermass (another name for the Feast of Innocents); adults would slap children with sticks to remind them of King Herod's massacre. There are all sorts of obvious problems with this tradition, and one of the main reasons I disagree with it is that it makes something tragic into a game. Children aren't really edified by this activity, and for crying out loud, you're hitting children!

Another take on remembering the massacre of the innocents would be to make it a day of mourning. When you read the story, it's hard not to let it cut you deeply. I have four little children, and I hold them closer when I read this story. The poetic passage from Jeremiah (see below) referenced in Matthew's gospel amplifies what Matthew cannot say himself: children are ruthlessly killed and mothers weep without comfort.

And cruelty and the suffering of children is often a stumbling block to those who don't really know Christ. I think of Ivan Karamazov in *The Brothers Karamazov* and his refusal to accept Orthodox Christianity because he cannot fathom how a loving God would allow the suffering of children. I think of the senseless school shootings that have happened in the last fifteen years. Or the loss of innumerable lives yet to be born. These are indeed deeply dark and seemingly chaotic events.

But it is not the end of the story. For the innocents or for Jesus.

The children who lose their lives at the hands of Herod save the life of the Prince of Peace who will one day be the ultimate sacrifice for all. To the reader, it may seem like the children are merely pawns in the great drama of the Christ story; the loss of many babies shows the scope of the evil which seeks Christ.

And yet Jesus, who spent much of his adult life with his eyes fixed on the cross he would be nailed to, welcomed children so completely into his arms: "Let the children come to me, and do not hinder them, for to such belongs the kingdom of God."

For Jesus' story, we see the power of evil in full force, trying with its most diabolical efforts to destroy the Christ-child, and it cannot do it.

So why do we celebrate a day that seems unfathomable? Jeremiah says in the verse after Rachel's lamentation the following: "keep your voice from weeping, and your eyes from tears, for there is a reward for your walk, declares the Lord, and they shall come back from the land of the enemy. There is hope for your future, declares the Lord, and your children shall come back to their own country."

We celebrate the welcoming of these many saints—the children who have come back to their real country— whose hearts are known and made fully with Christ in heaven.

We celebrate that the light overcomes the darkness; chaos and senselessness do not get the last word. The innocents' story is intertwined with Christ's story of the redemption of mankind. Their sweet short lives protected Christ's mission on earth.

We celebrate their unwilling death that allows Jesus' willing sacrifice on the cross—the sacrifice to change death to life for all.

We celebrate the hope through Christ that one day we'll know these children, too. And that we'll meet with joy and laughter all those children who have been lost to us.

ACTIVITIES

Choose an activity that reminds you of your childhood, such as baking cookies or going for an adventure outdoors. Bring members of your household along.

- Visit a friend who has recently given birth, and make a dinner or baked goods for her and her family.
- Find out how best to pray for or help suffering children in poorer areas of the world or how to help out at a pregnancy center.

GIFT GIVING

- Give a gift of something comfortable and soft, i. e., a blanket, nice pajamas.
- Give a gift of something that reminds the recipient of his or her childhood
- NO CASH OPTION: Offer to give a gift of relaxation of some sort—a back massage or cleaning the kitchen so that your loved one can rest his or her feet.

LITERATURE

The Brothers Karamazov, Fyodor Dostoevsky

Taken from The Brothers Karamazov. *Ivan Karamazov is talking with his younger brother Alyosha about the problem of evil and why he cannot believe in a loving God.*

L isten! I took the case of children only to make my case clearer. Of the other tears of humanity with which the earth is soaked from its crust to its centre, I will say nothing. I have narrowed my subject on purpose. I am a bug, and I recognise in all humility that I cannot understand why the world is arranged as it is. Men are themselves to blame, I suppose; they were given paradise, they wanted freedom, and stole fire from heaven, though they knew they would become unhappy, so there is no need to pity them. With my pitiful, earthly, Euclidian understanding, all I know is that there is suffering and that there are none guilty; that cause follows effect, simply and directly; that everything flows and finds its level—but that's only Euclidian nonsense, I know that, and I can't consent to live by it! What comfort is it to me that there are none guilty and that cause follows effect simply and directly, and that I know it?—I must have justice, or I will destroy myself. And not justice in some remote infinite time and space, but here on earth, and that I could see myself. I have believed in it. I want to see it, and if I am dead by then, let me rise again, for if it all happens without me, it will be too unfair. Surely I haven't suffered simply that I, my crimes and my sufferings, may manure the soil of the future harmony for somebody else. I want to see with my own eyes the hind lie down with the lion and the victim rise up and embrace his murderer. I want to be there when everyone suddenly understands what it has all been for. All the religions of the world are built on this longing, and I am a believer. But then there are the children, and what am I to do about them? That's a question I can't answer. For the hundredth time I repeat, there are numbers of questions, but I've only taken the children, because in their case what I mean is so unanswerably clear. Listen! If all must suffer to pay for the eternal harmony, what have children to do with it, tell me, please? It's beyond all comprehension why they should suffer, and why they should pay for the harmony. Why should they, too, furnish material to enrich the soil for the harmony of the future? I understand solidarity in sin among men. I understand solidarity in retribution, too; but there can be no such solidarity with children. And if it is really true that they must share responsibility for all their fathers' crimes, such a truth is not of this world and is beyond my comprehension. Some jester will say, perhaps, that the child would have grown up and have sinned, but you see he didn't grow up, he was torn to pieces by the dogs, at eight years old. Oh, Alyosha, I am not blaspheming! I understand, of course, what an upheaval of the universe it will be when everything in heaven and earth blends in one hymn of praise and everything that lives and has lived cries aloud: 'Thou art just, O Lord, for Thy ways are revealed.' When the mother embraces the fiend who threw her child to the dogs, and all three cry aloud with tears, 'Thou art just, O Lord!' then, of course, the crown of knowledge will be reached and all will be made clear. But what pulls me up here is that I can't accept that harmony. And while I am on earth, I make haste to take my own measures. You see, Alyosha, perhaps it really may happen that if I live to that moment, or rise again to see it, I, too, perhaps, may cry aloud with the rest, looking at the mother embracing the child's torturer, 'Thou art just, O Lord!' but I don't want to cry aloud then. While there is still time, I hasten to protect myself, and so I renounce the higher harmony altogether. It's not worth the tears of that one tortured child who beat itself on the breast with its little fist and prayed in its stinking outhouse, with its unexpiated tears to 'dear, kind God'! It's not worth it, because those tears are unatoned for. They must be atoned for, or there can be no harmony. But how? How are you going to atone for them? Is it possible? By their being avenged? But what do I care for avenging them? What do I care for a hell for oppressors? What good can hell do, since those children have already been tortured? And what becomes of harmony, if there is hell? I want to forgive. I want to embrace. I don't want more suffering. And if the sufferings of children go to swell the sum of sufferings which was necessary to pay for truth, then I protest that the truth is not worth such a price. I don't want the mother to embrace the oppressor who threw her son to the dogs! She dare not forgive him! Let her forgive him for herself, if she will, let her forgive the torturer for the immeasurable suffering of her mother's heart. But the sufferings of her tortured child she has no right to forgive; she dare not forgive the torturer, even if the child were to forgive him! And if that is so, if they dare not forgive, what becomes of harmony? Is there in the whole world a being who would have the right to forgive and could forgive? I don't want harmony. From love for humanity I don't want it. I would rather be left with the unavenged suffering. I would rather remain with my unavenged suffering and unsatisfied indignation, even if I were wrong. Besides, too high a price is asked for harmony; it's beyond our means to pay so much to enter on it. And so I hasten to give back my entrance ticket, and if I am an honest man I am bound to give it back as soon as possible. And that I am doing. It's not God that I don't accept, Alyosha, only I most respectfully return him the ticket."

"That's rebellion," murmured Alyosha, looking down.

SCRIPTURE

Exodus 1; Jeremiah 31:1-36; Matthew 2:1-18;
Luke 18:15-17

JOURNAL PROMPTS

What point is Jesus trying to make when he says, "Let the little children come to me, for the Kingdom of Heaven belongs to such as these," as well as the other statements where he holds up children as a model of faith?

Think of a time God has comforted you in the midst of grief and tragedy and write about it. How did he comfort you?

In the literature for today, Ivan Karamazov "refuses to be comforted" regarding the death and suffering of children, much like Rachel in the passage quoted in Matthew. To what extent is this refusal good? At what point (if ever) does it become bad?

CAROLS

"Silent Night"
"The Coventry Carol"

The Fifth Day

The Feast of St. Thomas Becket

Almighty God, you gave your servant Thomas Becket boldness to confess the Name of our Savior Jesus Christ before the rulers of this world, and courage to die for this faith: Grant that we may always be ready to give a reason for the hope that is in us, and to suffer gladly for the sake of our Lord Jesus Christ; who lives and reigns with you and the Holy Spirit, one God, for ever and ever. Amen.

—*The Book of Common Prayer*

REFLECTION

Since the time of Christ, the World has always attacked the Church in one of two ways. Sensible, cynical, well-meaning tyrants (as well as a few absolute stinkers) have tried either to annihilate the Church completely or to compromise its Gospel and use it for their own ends. They did this in Christ's day, they are doing it in ours, and we all often do play the part of Peter (or, if we're not careful, Judas) in selling Christ out to our persecutors or cultural allies in exchange for their esteem, our lives, comfort, control, or for ideals that we tell ourselves are inspired by our faith but actually have become religions of their own. Saint Thomas Becket is as relevant now as he has ever been.

Thomas Becket was appointed Archbishop of Canterbury in 1162 by Henry II, King of England. Until that point he had worked as Chancellor for Henry, who often (like many monarchs) engaged in power games with the Pope. The understanding at Thomas's appointment was that he would make some of these power games easier for Henry to win, but the opposite happened. It's quite possible that his appointment as Archbishop caused him to take his duties—and his God—suddenly quite seriously, in a way he possibly had not before. He resigned his position as Chancellor (which he'd been expected to keep along with his Archbishopric). The two men were drawn into a feud that resulted in Thomas being exiled and Henry's allies excommunicated, until (on this day in A.D. 1170) Henry "accidentally" had his old friend assassinated. Inside his church. At the altar.

The optics of this sacrilege were not so great for Henry, and the upshot of it all was that he had to eat crow and acknowledge Thomas as a saint; the four knights who did the murdering, meanwhile, were excommunicated. The Pope (who, it should be said, often himself played the part of the cynical, well-meaning tyrant) had won this round. But I think that, whatever Becket's motives, his story can remind us that it is possible to refuse worldly power. There was no obvious reason for him to give up his power, much less his life.

We are interested in power these days and suspicious of stories of altruism (of course, the martyrs are not really altruists but people who believe that the fulfillment of their deepest desires is only possible after death). Yet even our insistence that everyone is really looking for earthly power tends to run aground in the face of martyrdom. The multitude of people who have been willing to lose their lives rather than receive worldly power or security tends to undermine the secularist assumptions that most of the time seem like common sense. The king Becket chooses over Henry II really does seem to be Christ, who (while of the royal line of David) was born as a commoner and consistently refused worldly power each time it was offered. The miracle of the Incarnation redeems the nature of authority itself. It's a commonplace that in seeking power, tyrants and rulers in essence become slaves. Desiring power over others means your worth—in your own eyes—is measured by their high or low opinion of you. Classical philosophers have noted that the tyrant is thus the unhappiest and most insecure person of all, because he must constantly hoard or expand his supposed power in order to retain his sense of self.

But Christ, the true King, does not play power games:

"Now when he was in Jerusalem at the Passover Feast, many believed in his name when they saw the signs that he was doing. But Jesus on his part did not entrust himself to them, because he knew all people and needed no one to bear witness about man, for he himself knew what was in man." (John 2:23-25 ESV)

Or, again:

"Jesus, knowing that the Father had given all things into his hands, and that he had come from God and was going back to God, rose from supper. He laid aside his outer garments, and taking a towel, tied it around his waist." (John 13:3-4 ESV)

Kings and worldly rulers are little imperfect images of God's authority. But Christ's authority is independent from anyone's opinion of him, having everything to do with the relationship with the Father that he makes manifest—and accessible—to us. Our own dealings with the civil and cultural authorities of this world can be transformed. Even people in power can be transformed. But in the meantime, we need not be surprised, or even offended, when they oppose us. We have been told that they will. We can even have compassion on them when they persecute us, or when they try to use us, and we can pray for them as we deny them the slavery they desire. Serving the only real King, we can be free, like Thomas, to be "naive"—to say what is true and do what is right, even when it seems to cost us our lives.

ACTIVITIES

Get in touch with your inner Anglophile and do something British. Never had plum pudding? Now's the time to look up the recipe and try it. If you haven't already, go online and watch the King's first Christmas Day speech. Locate some Christmas crackers or eat fish and chips. (This may not be as meaningful if you live in the UK.)

- Consider and meditate on the nature of power and leadership. What makes a good Christian leader?
- Watch or read *Murder in the Cathedral* by T. S. Eliot. Alternatively, read the play together.
- Watch *A Man for All Seasons,* a story about a different King Henry and a different Thomas, but with some fascinating parallels to the saint's story we consider today.
- Group Activity: In honor of Chaucer's *Canterbury Tales* (about a story contest during a pilgrimage to Becket's shrine) spend time writing a one-page story on a piece of paper. It can be based on a story you've heard elsewhere, but add your own touches to it. Next, sit in a circle and write a short description of the life and/ or appearance of the person to your right (about a paragraph). Once you've all done this, read each others' stories out loud and then try to match the description of someone with the story they wrote. Finally, vote on the best story and give the winner some food as a prize. For an extra challenge, feel free to do all of the above in verse.
- Spend time in prayer for leaders, both in the Church and throughout the world.

GIFT GIVING

- Give one of the gifts you did not give on Christmas Day.
- "Relic" gift: Give a gift to someone else that will remind them of you or of someone (especially someone who has passed on) that you both want to remember.
- NO CASH OPTION: Make five golden rings to give to five of your friends (and then secretly forge a ruling ring to bend their will to yours). Just kidding. Find something outside that is blooming (or still green/colorful) and give it as a gift, along with written-out wishes for the coming year.

LITERATURE

Psalm 52 *by Mary Sidney Herbert*

Tyrant, why swell'st thou thus,
Of mischief vaunting?
Since help from God to us
Is never wanting.

Lewd lies thy tongue contrives,
Loud lies it soundeth;
Sharper than sharpest knives
With lies it woundeth.

Falsehood thy wit approves,
All truth rejected:
Thy will all vices loves,
Virtue neglected.

Not words from cursed thee,
But gulfs are poured;
Gulfs wherein daily be
Good men devoured.

Think'st thou to bear it so?
God shall displace thee;
God shall thee overthrow,
Crush thee, deface thee.

The just shall fearing see
These fearful chances,
And laughing shoot at thee
With scornful glances.

Lo, lo, the wretched wight,
Who God disdaining,
His mischief made his might,
His guard his gaining.

I as an olive tree
Still green shall flourish:
God's house the soil shall be
My roots to nourish.

My trust in his true love
Truly attending,
Shall never thence remove,
Never see ending.

Thee will I honour still,
Lord, for this justice;
There fix my hopes I will
Where thy saints' trust is.

Thy saints trust in thy name,
Therein they joy them:
Protected by the same,
Naught can annoy them.

SCRIPTURE

I Samuel 8, Isaiah 7:10-25, Psalm 72, Acts 4, Matthew 1

JOURNAL PROMPTS

How are people on the opposite side of the political aisle tempted to sell Christ out to persecutors or cultural allies? How are people on your side tempted to do the same? What about you yourself?

Do you agree with Plato that the tyrant is the unhappiest and most insecure person of all? How can we practice compassion toward them without enabling them?

How does remembering Christ's true kingdom and our citizenship in heaven allow us to stand up against tyranny?

CAROLS

"What Child Is This?"
"The Holly and the Ivy"

The Sixth Day

The Feast of the Holy Family

Almighty God, our heavenly Father, who set the solitary in families: We commend to your continual care the homes in which your people dwell. Put far from them, we beseech you, every root of bitterness, the desire of vainglory, and the pride of life. Fill them with faith, virtue, knowledge, temperance, patience, godliness. Knit together in constant affection those who, in holy wedlock, have been made one flesh. Turn the hearts of the parents to the children, and the hearts of the children to the parents; and so enkindle fervent charity among us all, that we may evermore be kindly affectioned one to another; through Jesus Christ our Lord. Amen.

—*The Book of Common Prayer*

REFLECTION

So here's a yuletide newsflash: Christmas is probably not about spending time with your family. I realize that such a statement flies in the face of a century or so of accumulated commercial Christmas wisdom—the hundreds of inoffensive plays, television specials, and songs where a family finds the "true meaning of Christmas" after losing its source of income, and as a result its members learn to appreciate each other. I'm not saying this is a bad thing to learn. Obviously, relationships do make us happier than getting stuff, and families are important and good. But the effect of this repeated message is to intensify the loneliness of those who are—for whatever reason—

separated from their own families at Christmas. Not only have their loved ones been taken from them, but so has (if the holiday specials are right) an essential aspect of Christmas.

Obviously, it's good to spend time with your family during Christmas, if you have one. It's probably even your duty. But Christmas is not really about your family, any more than it's about your presents. We want both but can do without them if necessary.

Instead, Christmas is about how a transcendent and immutable God became our family and gave us his own. This is a gift that all people are in need of, whether they already have a family or not. And it is a gift that God gives throughout the year—though it is possible that Christmas, with its potential darkness, loneliness, and time off from ordinary routine, might make us more aware of our need for it. If this is you, take courage. Your heartbreak very well may be a prelude to fulfillment and wholeness beyond that experienced by most human beings. Draw near, and ask him to draw even nearer.

The Feast Day of the Holy Family is a comparatively recent feast day, and it is mainly celebrated by Roman Catholics. But I think all Christians can benefit from remembrance of the Holy Family, as surely as they can all benefit from a Methodist hymn like "Hark, the Herald Angels Sing" or an Anglican devotional writer like C. S. Lewis. The original idea behind the feast (begun in the 17th Century) is that Christians should use the Holy Family (meaning Jesus, Mary, and Joseph) as a pattern for their own families.

Initially, this sounds misguided, especially to cynical moderns. It sounds a bit like the well-meaning Christmas carols that have lyrics like: And through all His wondrous childhood / He would honor and obey, / Love and watch the lowly maiden, / In whose gentle arms He lay: / Christian children all must be / Mild, obedient, good as He. /For he is our childhood's pattern..." (From "Once in Royal David's City").

The whole thing sounds like a watered-down variant of the Adoptionist heresy: "Be good, like Jesus (or Mary) was, and God will adopt you too. Make sure to be a perfect, attractive member of a perfect, attractive family." Yet it's important to note that, in Scripture, while Jesus, Mary, and Joseph were characterized by their wholehearted response to God, the descriptions we get of their interactions—I mean the ones drawn from the Gospels rather than from imagination or legend—are complex, full of wrinkles, and by no means cheap. Joseph plans to break off his betrothal to Mary (essentially, to divorce her) when he finds out she is pregnant with Jesus; they have to run away to Egypt; they lose Jesus when he is twelve, and when they catch up with him, he essentially rebukes them and alludes to the fact that Joseph is not his real dad; when he grows up, according to John 7, "not even his brothers believe[ ] in him"; critics of his ministry call him a Samaritan, alluding to his potentially non-Jewish parentage; and when people do tell him, "Blessed is the womb that bore you and the breasts that gave you suck," Jesus himself responds, "Blessed rather are those who know and do the will of God." To top it all off, while he makes arrangements for Mary from the cross (last minute, anyone?), Jesus' manner of death brings lasting shame upon her and her late husband. Only the Resurrection changes it all, and likely most of Mary's acquaintances, neighbors, and extended family didn't even believe. There is nothing especially tidy or obviously exemplary, in other words, about the Holy Family. This complexity is part of the reason I love the above painting. They are fleeing to Egypt, and they look a bit like they're quarreling: Joseph keeping his distance from Mary and looking sheepish, while she looks downright peeved with him about something. Presumably, no one besides the viewer of the painting is able to see their halos, marking them out as saintly. And yet the halos are there.

If they are the least dysfunctional family ever, they have a funny way of showing it. But they are exemplary, all the same, and more than exemplary. Joseph does plan to divorce Mary at first, but he does what he can to reduce scandal for the sake of a woman who (as far as he knows) has betrayed him. He decides to marry her anyway in response to a dream. He could have turned over, gone back to sleep, and had a conventional, easy, stable (so to speak) family life with someone else, but he decided to believe the dream actually was a message from God. Mary, meanwhile, could have responded to God's invitation with a simple "No thanks!" She could have refused to become God's family, preferring instead her own good reputation and uncomplicated life. Jesus, meanwhile, could have done everything his earthly parents (who were not omniscient) expected of him, but he did his Father's will instead.

All three of them, as I said before, were characterized by a wholehearted response to God. And, in fact, I believe they did love each other and serve each other, because it is only when human beings give priority to the transcendent—to God himself—that they are able to stop idolizing human relationships. They are, paradoxically, more free to give themselves to each other when they are themselves centered on God. But they will rarely fit the image other people have of "the perfect family" when they do. They will be better, though not everyone will recognize their oddly tilting halos, aligned with heaven's horizon rather than earth's.

They, of course, are not only a model but a gift to us. Jesus' mother and earthly father become ours as well ("Son, behold thy Mother"). And his brothers—all believers—become our brothers too. Even if those on this side of death so often forget it, it's a fact, and we can love them like brothers. Most of all, he is able to give us his own family because he first gives us his true Father, and we are fully adopted, wrinkles, complications, and all. Our ultimate Holy Family is the Holy Trinity; the love existing between the Father, Son, and Holy Spirit that is at its heart transmutes our very selves and our relationships into a particular and peculiar sanctity. The Father, Son, and Holy Spirit, always relating to one another in mutual delight, draw us to their table to, in George Herbert's words, "sit and eat." And the amazing thing is that this is a gift to us not only from the Trinity but also from his family on earth, whose choice of the Perfect made them so apparently flawed, yet so very fulfilled.

ACTIVITIES

If possible, spend time with family, prioritizing them over work, hobbies, social media, etc.

- Handwrite a few thank-you notes for the Christmas gifts you've received so far, and send them.
- Take some time to meditate on Rublev's "Holy Trinity" icon.
- Pore over a few of the phrases in the Chesterton poem on the next page.
- What does it mean that "Men are homesick in their homes"? What in the world is Chesterton talking about?

GIFT GIVING

- Give one of the gifts you did not give on Christmas Day.
- Print photos and make someone a scrapbook featuring family members or other people you both knew or know.
- Buy or create a visual or verbal devotional aid for someone else—a devotional poem, icon, illustrated Scripture verse, etc.
- NO CASH OPTION: Write a note of appreciation (or song) to a family member, commenting on how their specific personality (completely unique) has fit them for the particular role they have played in your life (as son, father, mother, husband, wife, etc.).

LITERATURE

"A Christmas Poem" by G. K. Chesterton

There fared a mother driven forth
Out of an inn to roam;
In the place where she was homeless
All men are at home.
The crazy stable close at hand,
With shaking timber and shifting sand,
Grew a stronger thing to abide and stand
Than the square stones of Rome.

For men are homesick in their homes,
And strangers under the sun,
And they lay their heads in a foreign land
Whenever the day is done.

Here we have battle and blazing eyes,
And chance and honour and high surprise,
But our homes are under miraculous skies
Where the yule tale was begun.

A child in a foul stable,
Where the beasts feed and foam;
Only where He was homeless
Are you and I at home;
We have hands that fashion and heads that know,
But our hearts we lost—how long ago!
In a place no chart nor ship can show Under the sky's dome.

This world is wild as an old wife's tale,
And strange the plain things are,
The earth is enough and the air is enough
For our wonder and our war;
But our rest is as far as the fire-drake swings
And our peace is put in impossible things
Where clashed and thundered unthinkable wings
Round an incredible star.

To an open house in the evening
Home shall all men come,
To an older place than Eden
And a taller town than Rome.
To the end of the way of the wandering star,
To the things that cannot be and that are,
To the place where God was homeless
And all men are at home.

SCRIPTURE

Ruth 1, Psalm 146, Ephesians 5:15-6:4, Luke 2:41-52

JOURNAL PROMPTS

Think about a character from the Bible who did not have an ideal home life, and meditate on their story a bit. How did God meet them despite (or because of) their family's dysfunction?

How is God offering to become your family this year?

What do you think Chesterton means when he says in today's poem, "Men are homesick in their homes"?

What are some ways you can extend the invitation to become God's family to others?

CAROLS

"Nowell Sing Thee"
"O Little Town of Bethlehem"

The Seventh Day

Eve of The Holy Name of Jesus; New Year's Eve

Accept, O Lord, our thanks and praise for all that you have done for us. We thank you for the splendor of the whole creation, for the beauty of this world, for the wonder of life, and for the mystery of love. We thank you for the blessing of family and friends, and for the loving care which surrounds us on every side. We thank you for setting us at tasks which demand our best efforts, and for leading us to accomplishments which satisfy and delight us. We thank you also for those disappointments and failures that lead us to acknowledge our dependence on you alone. Above all, we thank you for your Son Jesus Christ; for the truth of his Word and the example of his life; for his steadfast obedience, by which he overcame temptation; for his dying, through which he overcame death; and for his rising to life again, in which we are raised to the life of your kingdom. Grant us the gift of your Spirit, that we may know Christ and make him known; and through him, at all times and in all places, may give thanks to you in all things.

—*The Book of Common Prayer*

REFLECTION

Most traditional cultures, even those deeply informed by Christianity, have believed in the idea of luck and have attempted to improve that luck through rituals of various kinds. These actions seem unenlightened to us, but they're really the same impulse (desire to control our fate in a world that is often beyond our control) that has given us most forms of modern science and technology. Our methods have improved, but our aims are similar.

Now that they are disproven or supplanted, New Year rituals like eating a pig to ensure prosperity in the coming year or beans to secure good harvest are charming to us, and I do not see much harm in practicing them for nostalgia's sake. But I expect for some of the original practitioners (and for some still today), these rituals carried with them the earnestness that many of us reserve for New Year's resolutions, one of the means by which we now attempt to make certain that the following year will be a good one. Having a good harvest has been replaced by resolving to change your habits to get a good job; hopes of marriage or childbirth in the coming year have been replaced by visits to the gym to ultimately win approval of someone else or health for yourself. These modern good luck rituals are less superstitious in that actually changing our habits is more likely to change our short-term destiny—but the desire to control is still there in all its humorless angst and deep drive to create a perfect world for ourselves.

So is the significance we attribute to a new year. Why should the practical tools we have for marking time—themselves necessary but arbitrary, be imbued with some sort of mystical significance? Going to the gym or on a new diet the first week of the new year (as opposed to any other time) is not so different, in this sense, from older, more inscrutable rituals. Both give us a kind of hope by consolidating past and present behaviors and events, separating them from an imagined future that is about to begin, and placing them mentally in the "past." We get to use the helpful labels "last year" and "this year," sending last year out of the camp as a kind of numerical scapegoat after pinning our personal and corporate evils to it. How many times have we groused about "the year" that has just "passed," contrasting it with what we hope the magical "New Year" will bring? This might be a helpful way to think, of course, but it is magical thinking all the same.

I was recently surprised to learn that hope itself was once considered akin to superstition. Most educated people in the Hellenic world, before the Advent of Christ, believed that hope was a delusion—one of the evils remaining in Pandora's box that made mortals feel the other evils all the more sharply. Harvest might be good this year, but the following year, starvation could be imminent. We won the war this time, but next time, our enemies will destroy us. Even if they didn't, of course, life would deteriorate into old age, disease, and death, as it still does. Hope was prelude to tragedy. The only sane response to such a mutable world was to take delight in those things that were already present and would not be so easily lost—ideas, virtues, traditions, the stars, the gods. But to hope for better fortune was bad philosophy.

The God of the Hebrews was different. He promised not only spiritual rewards to his followers but physical blessings to the nation of Israel. And when he became incarnate (so Christians believe) as Jesus, his message was not simply that people should stop hoping for good lives and focus on the eternal because they would die one day. He healed people's bodies, even if they would get sick again. He raised Lazarus, even though he knew he would die again. And he himself came back from death, claiming to have conquered it once and for all. This sounded crazy, like a superstition, to the educated people of Athens, who laughed at Paul when he tried to pass on the news of death's defeat. Paul had to insist that this hope "does not put us to shame." So important was hope that it became one of the three theological virtues besides faith and love, especially accessible to Christians.

So, how does hope in the Resurrection tie into our minor, personal hopes and superstitions? Can it redeem them? Can we twist the arm of God with our rituals? Does the Almighty, transcendent, immutable Omnipotence give a fig for our civic new year, our categories, our resolutions about fertility or harvest, fitness or work? I think the Incarnation, and Jesus' ministry, leaves us little room to doubt that he does. Every aspect of life, in fact, can be embraced with hearts full of hope, with love of God and neighbor, and with prayers of faith. Rather than living defensively, as if these mutable and seemingly limited aspects of our lives have nothing to do with God's Important Business, we can live in the sure knowledge that these things actually matter more to God than they do to us. Attempts to control our lives utterly are sinful, not because our lives do not matter, but because we refuse to believe that a God who died for us does not care about our day-to-day existence. Instead, he makes our lives manifestations of the eternal within time.

Each desire, each prayer, points us not merely to the impassive, eternal unchanging reality but to ultimate, embodied joy, in which all our earthly longings are fulfilled in the Resurrection.

This is why prayer and thanksgiving are such gifts to us. They acknowledge that the God of the Universe is not limited by his large size to care only about his own Important Business of running the cosmos (or even saving eternal souls). He is infinite, and he cares infinitely about the details of our lives. He commands us to pray for our daily bread and the coming of his kingdom and to thank him for the spiritual and material blessings of the day (or of the past year). We thus acknowledge that the universe is governed by someone who, while more than a person, is certainly not less than one. Each answered prayer becomes an icon of our own future Resurrection, some small manifestation of the restoration of all things. Each unanswered prayer, likewise, drives us to pray all the more for this same restoration, so that we are groaning along with creation for the true New Year that will come at the end of time. Thanksgiving allows us to acknowledge that God, not luck or fate, has given us what good we have, not because we have deserved it by being holy enough or praying enough or dieting or eating enough pork and beans on New Year's, but out of his goodness.

ACTIVITIES

Have a discussion: Look up other New Year's Eve/St. Sylvester traditions and have a conversation about the nature of luck. To what extent is the idea of luck compatible with Christianity (or with whatever beliefs, formal or informal, that you hold)? Can you make any sort of a case for it? What is the difference between luck, fortune, and chance? Buy and set off fireworks to mark the beginning of the New Year.

- If you have a pig, walk it on a leash (a tradition from Vienna). If you don't have a pig, don't steal one. Walk the dog instead.
- Compile a list of books you would like to read and projects you'd like to do in the next year.

- Spend time looking back over a calendar or pictures from the last year and talking about your favorite moments from each month.
- Invite friends or family over, and make a black-eyed peas dish called "Hoppin' John's," as is traditional in parts of the American South.
- Write a wish for the upcoming year, burn it, then (if you're especially hardcore) drink the ashes in your New Year's beverage of choice, as is traditional in parts of Russia.
- I like this idea from catholicculture.org: "On the eve of the civil New Year the children may join their parents in a holy hour, in prayer and thanksgiving for the gifts and benefits which God has given them in the past year, and to pray for necessary graces in the forthcoming civil year."

GIFT GIVING

- Give one of the gifts you did not give on the first day of Christmas.
- Give someone twelve envelopes labeled with the twelve months of the year, featuring a wish, a scripture, a picture, a quote, a poem that they can read the first day of each month this year (obviously, this is also appropriate for New Year's Day).
- NO CASH OPTION: Create a song, poem, or picture featuring what you think was the most important memory shared between you and the gift's recipient over the past year.

LITERATURE

"The Darkling Thrush" by Thomas Hardy

I leant upon a coppice gate
When Frost was spectre-grey,
And Winter's dregs made desolate
The weakening eye of day.
The tangled bine-stems scored the sky
Like strings of broken lyres,
And all mankind that haunted nigh

Had sought their household fires.
The land's sharp features seemed to be
The Century's corpse outleant,
His crypt the cloudy canopy,
The wind his death-lament.
The ancient pulse of germ and birth
Was shrunken hard and dry,
And every spirit upon earth
Seemed fervourless as I.

At once a voice arose among
The bleak twigs overhead
In a full-hearted evensong
Of joy illimited;
An aged thrush, frail, gaunt, and small,
In blast-beruffled plume,
Had chosen thus to fling his soul
Upon the growing gloom.

So little cause for carolings
Of such ecstatic sound
Was written on terrestrial things
Afar or nigh around,
That I could think there trembled through
His happy good-night air
Some blessed Hope, whereof he knew
And I was unaware.

SCRIPTURE

Deuteronomy 8, Isaiah 65, Psalm 148,
Romans 7-8, John 8

JOURNAL PROMPTS

What are some of your modern good-luck rituals that you tend to practice in order to more effectively control your life when the new year comes? Which should you cast aside? Which can you infuse with the truth of the Gospel?

What were some of the things God has revealed to you in the past year about himself? If you don't have a ready answer, take time to pray and consider the question.

What are some things you'd like to see happen in the next year? Feel free to list spiritual desires here, but don't hide from God your seemingly "non-spiritual" goals, hopes, and ambitions. At the same time, this ain't magic or a vision board—it's a relationship. Just be honest about what you want.

CAROLS

"Adam Lay Ybounden"
"O Holy Night"

The Eighth Day

Solemnity of the Mary the Mother of God
THE FIRST DAY OF THE NEW YEAR

Eternal Father, who didst give to thine incarnate Son the holy name of Jesus to be the sign of our salvation: Plant in every heart, we beseech thee, the love of him who is the Savior of the world, even our Lord Jesus Christ; who liveth and reigneth with thee and the Holy Spirit, one God, in glory everlasting. Amen.

—*The Book of Common Prayer*

REFLECTION

It's fascinating to me when God bothers to command parents to give their children specific names. First, it seems strange that a name should matter at all to someone's destiny. Can't God achieve his purposes through someone, even if their name is not Jesus, or John, or Maher-shalal-hash-baz? I mean, the patriarchs of the twelve tribes of Israel were given joke names, for crying out loud, that alluded to the Great Conception Contest between Rachel and Leah, and they still managed to accomplish a good deal (namely, to become patriarchs and throw Joseph in a well so he could later save them from famine). The second odd thing about God telling Mary and Joseph what to name Jesus is that God could have pulled the right strings and pushed the right buttons in terms of Mary and Joseph's mental processes and upbringing, so that they simply arrived at the name "Jesus" naturally.

But he didn't. He instead wanted their cooperation and obedience in giving this tiny body an audible identifier.

When we've given our kids names, it's always reminded me a bit of that part at the beginning of *Peter Pan* where he's lost his shadow and can't put it back on, so Wendy has to sew it onto him. Even then, it's touch-and-go. He's not sure if it will take. Now here's this beautiful little miracle that you've known about for nine months but are just getting to know as a separate person, and you have the presumption to give it a label that never, at first, seems to stick. Later, of course, you can't think of the baby having any other name, but that's after they've really grown into it, and the man-made name has been fused irrevocably to the God-made baby. At first the name seems arbitrary, and the verbal stitch job you've just done of applying three (or more) names to this endlessly potential creature seems clumsy indeed. It is, in some ways, the first conscious effort you've made in marking a baby (which seems like a blank canvas) with the particular markings of your own culture. You've now taken an active role in tethering this natural thing to your particular civilization. I bet this is part of the reason that, in Jesus' culture, naming went along with circumcision. When you do either naming or circumcising, you are inflicting a particular cultural identity on someone that transcends this identity but is attached to and shaped by it all the same, and you are acknowledging that this eternal soul has a specific destiny.

In reality, of course, not only have you marked the child already (by speaking your language around him while he was in the womb, by eating certain foods, by passing your genes on), but the ideal, universal baby you hold has many of your own particular quirks, flaws, and virtues that are just waiting to manifest themselves. Now, the God of the Hebrews, who has refused to give himself a name other than I Am That I Am (despite permitting cultural shorthands that have become generic words for gods or nobility, such as "Elohim," "Lord," "Adonai," "God," "Deus,") has commanded that this bewildered couple name the Incarnate Word Itself! And the name "Jeshua" or Joshua in Hebrew is entirely culturally conventional. There are other guys named Jesus mentioned, even in the Gospels.

Yet now the transcendent, absolute Principle of Life has addressed himself to human beings, using the name "Jesus," which in his chosen, particular culture links him with Joshua (who, as the successor of Moses, led Israel into the Promised Land) and also means "one who saves." So Yahweh, whose name in Hebrew is basically "Don't try to label me because I'm not small enough for your categories," has given himself a particular identity that aligns with his function relative to Israel (and, as it happens, to all humanity): "You will call his name Jesus, for he will save his people from their sins." God the Son, existing before eternity in Trinity with the Father and the Spirit, is now named Jesus. In becoming Incarnate, he has drawn humanity up into the eternal Godhead and thus makes the particularities of Jesus' genes, Jesus' traditions, Jesus' languages into specific facets of Almighty God. Jesus' human, first-century Aramaic Jewishness and the salvation of humans are now a central aspect of the identity of God. It would be scandalous enough to treat these factors as means by which God has identified himself to us: "You finite people should think of Me, transcendent though I am, as a Jewish guy named Jesus because your tiny minds can't comprehend Me." But this "scandal of particularity," as it has been called, goes deeper: Because God exists as Trinity, in community, the specific cultural elements and mission are now part of the way Jesus is identified to the Father, through the Holy Spirit. God has, in other words, used human culture and categories—as well as Christ's own mission relative to humans—to identify himself to himself. The Son is "Jesus" not only to us but to the Father and Holy Spirit.

This brings us to Mary, the "Theotokos," the God-bearer, from whom Christ most directly took his humanity, his cultural and genetic heritage, and his name (she is called the God-bearer, by the way, not to imply that she herself is divine, but to emphasize the fact that Christ, whom she bore, is fully God). Her song of praise in Luke 1, the "Magnificat," is so well known, to the point that we often forget how culturally specific it is. It could be taken straight from the Psalms and could be interpreted along purely political lines. The list of things Mary announces that her child will do fits in perfectly with the expectations of the Jewish Messiah that were held during her time (and that cost Jesus many followers when he refused them). The Savior, the Jesus her song anticipates, will overthrow particular tyrants who oppress her own people in the present. I do not know if, at this time, she sees beyond this hope, to anticipate the means by which God will effect a transfiguration: How he will take a thoroughly

Jewish song like the "Magnificat," and a thoroughly Jewish figure like the Messiah and—through Mary's response—fulfill it in a way that transcends particulars and transforms humanity itself, destroying Death and Sin and allowing for all people to be adopted as sons and daughters of God.

For Jesus, while absolutely one with his culture, refused to allow that culture to limit the salvation he brought. Mary, born (as her Son was) of a particular people, voices longings that can ultimately be answered, not by a change of regime, but only by the regeneration worked in the hearts of her people and all people. And Mary, through whom Jesus is born, who assents to the Incarnation, who works with God to give to God a people and a name, becomes, in a sense, our own Jewish mother. For her Son draws us toward him, toward the fulfillment of the longings of every heart in every culture within the eternal exchange of love and life that exists in the Trinity. This fulfillment comes thanks to the marks he received at the rough hands of the Gentiles when he was named "King of the Jews." It is here that we receive our new marks, our new names.

ACTIVITIES

Decide to take up a hobby for the next twelve months and create a timetable to allow you to fit that hobby in among your other obligations.

- Arrange an impromptu brunch with family and/or friends.
- Go for a walk or a hike (weather permitting).
- Choose an organization or charity to give to consistently throughout the next twelve months.
- Look up New Year's Day parades that are being held in your own town or in local towns and attend one.

GIFT GIVING

- Give one of the gifts you did not give on the first day of Christmas.
- Give a book with a character who has an interesting name, a personalized gift or one that reminds you of your loved one's name.
- For Catholics, this may be a great day to give someone a rosary.
- Give someone a book you think they would enjoy this year.
- NO CASH OPTION: Create a "mixtape" (playlist) for someone else (a list on Spotify or Youtube, perhaps) featuring twelve songs, one for each month of the coming year.

LITERATURE
Taken from Peter Pan *by J.M. Barrie*
"Chapter 1: Peter Breaks Through"

All children, except one, grow up. They soon know that they will grow up, and the way Wendy knew was this. One day when she was two years old she was playing in a garden, and she plucked another flower and ran with it to her mother. I suppose she must have looked rather delightful, for Mrs. Darling put her hand to her heart and cried, "Oh, why can't you remain like this for ever!" This was all that passed between them on the subject, but henceforth Wendy knew that she must grow up. You always know after you are two. Two is the beginning of the end.

Of course they lived at 14 [their house number on the street], and until Wendy came, her mother was the chief one. She was a lovely lady, with a romantic mind and such a sweet mocking mouth. Her romantic mind was like the tiny boxes, one within the other, that come from the puzzling East, however many you discover there is always one more; and her sweet mocking mouth had one kiss on it that Wendy could never get, though there it was, perfectly conspicuous in the right-hand corner.

The way Mr. Darling won her was this: the many gentlemen who had been boys when she was a girl discovered simultaneously that they loved her, and they all ran to her house to propose to her except Mr. Darling, who took a cab and nipped in first, and so he got her. He got all of her, except the innermost box and the kiss. He never knew about the box, and in time he gave up trying for the kiss. Wendy thought Napoleon could have got it, but I can picture him trying and then going off in a passion, slamming the door.

Mr. Darling used to boast to Wendy that her mother not only loved him but respected him. He was one of those deep ones who know about stocks and shares. Of course no one really knows, but he quite seemed to know, and he often said stocks were up and shares were down in a way that would have made any woman respect him.

Mrs. Darling was married in white, and at first she kept the books perfectly, almost gleefully, as if it were a game, not so much as a Brussels sprout was missing; but by and by whole cauliflowers dropped out, and instead of them there were pictures of babies without faces. She drew them when she should have been totting up. They were Mrs. Darling's guesses.

Wendy came first, then John, then Michael.

For a week or two after Wendy came it was doubtful whether they would be able to keep her, as she was another mouth to feed. Mr. Darling was frightfully proud of her, but he was very honourable, and he sat on the edge of Mrs. Darling's bed, holding her hand and calculating expenses, while she looked at him imploringly. She wanted to risk it, come what might, but that was not his way; his way was with a pencil and a piece of paper, and if she confused him with suggestions, he had to begin at the beginning again.

"Now don't interrupt," he would beg of her.

"I have one pound seventeen here, and two and six at the office; I can cut off my coffee at the office, say ten shillings, making two nine and six, with your eighteen and three makes three nine seven, with five naught naught in my cheque-book makes eight nine seven—who is that moving?—eight nine seven, dot and carry seven—don't speak, my own—and the pound you lent to that man who came to the door—quiet, child—dot and carry child—there, you've done it!—did I say nine nine seven? yes, I said nine nine seven; the question is, can we try it for a year on nine nine seven?"

"Of course we can, George," she cried. But she was prejudiced in Wendy's favour, and he was really the grander character of the two.

"Remember mumps," he warned her almost threateningly, and off he went again. "Mumps one pound, that is what I have put down, but I daresay it will be more like thirty shillings—don't speak—measles one five, German measles half a guinea, makes two fifteen six—don't waggle your finger—whooping-cough, say fifteen shillings"—and so on it went, and it added up differently each time; but at last Wendy just got through, with mumps reduced to twelve six, and the two kinds of measles treated as one.

There was the same excitement over John, and Michael had even a narrower squeak; but both were kept, and soon, you might have seen the three of them going in a row to Miss Fulsom's Kindergarten school, accompanied by their nurse.

Mrs. Darling loved to have everything just so, and Mr. Darling had a passion for being exactly like his neighbours; so, of course, they had a nurse. As they were poor, owing to the amount of milk the children drank, this nurse was a prim Newfoundland dog, called Nana, who had belonged to no one in particular until the Darlings engaged her. She had always thought children important, however, and the Darlings had become acquainted with her in Kensington Gardens, where she spent most of her spare time peeping into perambulators, and was much hated by careless nursemaids, whom she followed to their homes and complained of to their mistresses. She proved to be quite a treasure of a nurse. How thorough she was at bath-time, and up at any moment of the night if one of her charges made the slightest cry. Of course her kennel was in the nursery. She had a genius for knowing when a cough is a thing to have no patience with and when it needs stocking around your throat. She believed to her last day in old-fashioned remedies like rhubarb leaf and made sounds of contempt over all this new-fangled talk about germs and so on. It was a lesson in propriety to see her escorting the children to school, walking sedately by their side when they were well behaved and butting them back into line if they strayed. On John's footer days she never once forgot his sweater, and she usually carried an umbrella in her mouth in case of rain. There is a room in the basement of Miss Fulsom's school where the nurses wait. They sat on forms, while Nana lay on the floor, but that was the only difference. They affected to ignore her as of an inferior social status to themselves, and she despised their light talk. She resented visits to the nursery from Mrs. Darling's friends, but if they did come, she first whipped off Michael's pinafore and put him into the one with blue braiding and smoothed out Wendy and made a dash at John's hair.

No nursery could possibly have been conducted more correctly, and Mr. Darling knew it, yet he sometimes wondered uneasily whether the neighbours talked.

He had his position in the city to consider.

Nana also troubled him in another way. He had sometimes a feeling that she did not admire him. "I know she admires you tremendously, George," Mrs. Darling would assure him, and then she would sign to the children to be specially nice to father. Lovely dances followed, in which the only other servant, Liza, was sometimes allowed to join. Such a midget she looked in her long skirt and maid's cap, though she had sworn, when engaged, that she would never see ten again. The gaiety of those romps! And gayest of all was Mrs. Darling, who would pirouette so wildly that all you could see of her was the kiss, and then if you had dashed at her you might have got it. There never was a simpler happier family until the coming of Peter Pan.

Mrs. Darling first heard of Peter when she was tidying up her children's minds. It is the nightly custom of every good mother after her children are asleep to rummage in their minds and put things straight for next morning, repacking into their proper places the many articles that have wandered during the day. If you could keep awake (but of course you can't), you would see your own mother doing this, and you would find it very interesting to watch her. It is quite like tidying up drawers. You would see her on her knees, I expect, lingering humorously over some of your contents, wondering where on earth you had picked this thing up, making discoveries sweet and not so sweet, pressing this to her cheek as if it were as nice as a kitten and hurriedly stowing that out of sight. When you wake in the morning, the naughtiness and evil passions with which you went to bed have been folded up small and placed at the bottom of your mind and on the top, beautifully aired, are spread out your prettier thoughts, ready for you to put on.

I don't know whether you have ever seen a map of a person's mind. Doctors sometimes draw maps of other parts of you, and your own map can become intensely interesting, but catch them trying to draw a map of a child's mind, which is not only confused, but keeps going round all the time. There are zigzag lines on it, just like your temperature on a card, and these are probably roads in the island, for the Neverland is always more or less an island, with astonishing splashes of colour here and there, and coral reefs and rakish-looking craft in the offing and savages and lonely lairs and gnomes who are mostly tailors and caves through which a river runs and princes with six elder brothers and a hut fast going to decay and one very small old lady with a hooked nose. It would be an easy map if that were all, but there is also first day at school, religion, fathers, the round pond, needle-work, murders, hangings, verbs that take the dative, chocolate pudding day, getting into braces, say ninety-nine, three-pence for pulling out your tooth yourself, and so on, and either these are part of the island or they are another map showing through, and it is all rather confusing, especially as nothing will stand still.

Of course the Neverlands vary a good deal. John's, for instance, had a lagoon with flamingoes flying over it at which John was shooting, while

Michael, who was very small, had a flamingo with lagoons flying over it. John lived in a boat turned upside down on the sands, Michael in a wigwam, Wendy in a house of leaves deftly sewn together. John had no friends, Michael had friends at night, Wendy had a pet wolf forsaken by its parents, but on the whole the Neverlands have a family resemblance, and if they stood still in a row you could say of them that they have each other's nose, and so forth. On these magic shores children at play are for ever beaching their coracles. We too have been there; we can still hear the sound of the surf, though we shall land no more.

Of all delectable islands the Neverland is the snuggest and most compact, not large and sprawly, you know, with tedious distances between one adventure and another, but nicely crammed. When you play at it by day with the chairs and table-cloth, it is not in the least alarming, but in the two minutes before you go to sleep it becomes very real. That is why there are night-lights.

Occasionally in her travels through her children's minds Mrs. Darling found things she could not understand, and of these quite the most perplexing was the word *Peter*. She knew of no Peter, and yet he was here and there in John and Michael's minds, while Wendy's began to be scrawled all over with him. The name stood out in bolder letters than any of the other words, and as Mrs. Darling gazed, she felt that it had an oddly cocky appearance.

"Yes, he is rather cocky," Wendy admitted with regret. Her mother had been questioning her.

"But who is he, my pet?"

"He is Peter Pan, you know, mother."

At first Mrs. Darling did not know, but after thinking back into her childhood, she just remembered a Peter Pan who was said to live with the fairies. There were odd stories about him, as that when children died he went part of the way with them, so that they should not be frightened. She had believed in him at the time, but now that she was married and full of sense, she quite doubted whether there was any such person.

"Besides," she said to Wendy, "he would be grown up by this time."

To meet Peter Pan and his shadow, continue reading to chapter 2.
The entire novel of Peter Pan is in the public domain, which can be found online.

SCRIPTURE

Exodus 3, Isaiah 9, Psalm 118, Phillipians 2:1–18

JOURNAL PROMPTS

How else (besides names) do we mark our children or ourselves with the particularities of our culture? Should we resist such markings as limiting, or should we embrace them as gifts?

Why do you think God bothered to insist that Mary name their Son Jesus? Couldn't he save his people from their sins if his name was Samuel or Saul or Judah?

Spend some time meditating on Mary's prophetic psalm, the "Magnificat." What does it reveal about who Christ is?

CAROLS

"For Unto Us a Child is Born"
"There Is No Rose of Such Virtue"

The Ninth Day

Feast of St. Basil & St. Gregory of Nazianzen

Almighty Father, whose blessed Son before his passion prayed for his disciples that they might be one, as you and he are one: Grant that your Church, being bound together in love and obedience to you, may be united in one body by the one Spirit, that the world may believe in him whom you have sent, your Son Jesus Christ our Lord; who lives and reigns with you, in the unity of the Holy Spirit, one God, now and for ever.

—*The Book of Common Prayer*

REFLECTION

At one point or another in life, if you are not very careful, you will probably find yourself associated with a school play. This is especially true if you are in school, as I was at some indistinct point between the eighties and nineties when Culpeper Christian Elementary and Middle School staged a Christmas musical about a family who went somewhere or other for Christmas but forgot to bring presents and learned in the end that the presents were not as important as they thought.

Now, the weird thing is that I forget how I was involved. I'm pretty sure I wasn't acting in the play, which means I was either in the choir or band. I remember singing or maybe just hearing the songs several times and can to this day repeat the lyrics from such notable pieces as "You Can't Have Christmas Without Presents" and "Christmas Is a Time to Love." As far as I can remember, this play taught us basically the same thing we would have learned if we had stayed home and watched *Garfield's Christmas* or *National Lampoon's Christmas* on TV—albeit with fewer good jokes and a Jesus-y veneer that justified the whole endeavor to the well-meaning, patient adults behind the curtain and in the audience. And they say Christians don't suffer for their art.

All that to say, it is interesting how anti-consumerist most Christmas movies, specials, songs, plays, rock operas, and other productions tend to be. Christmas, they all maintain, is not about gifts. It's about people.

And that sort of sentiment, coming around this time of year, would be absolutely lovely and meaningful and welcome if we didn't all know in our heart of hearts that it was completely wrong.

Christmas is about presents.

There, I said it. Now, let me explain.

The choice between loved ones and presents is a false choice because gifts, when they work the right way, reinforce bonds between people.

I don't mean gifts are more important than the people who give them to you or even that Christmas is chiefly a time in which you are showered with all the stuff you want. In fact, a big part of what we want to do with Twelve Tide is to empower people to make their Christmas less consumerist and more meaningful.

The choice isn't really between stuff and people, but rather between giving and not giving. Even in *A Christmas Carol,* Ebenezer Scrooge is not so much condemned for being greedy as for being a miser. He wants to hoard his money. To spend it on gifts—and receive gifts in turn—is to become vulnerable to others and to spend time and resources on relationships rather than self-determination.

Scrooge has a literary ancestor named Heremod in the poem *Beowulf.* He is a king everyone in the poem knows about who once (before Beowulf's time) refused to give gifts and came to a bad end as a result. After young Beowulf risks his life for King Hrothgar (and is given lots of presents in return), the king tells him not to be like Heremod, who hoarded his treasure rather than giving it out freely. In *Beowulf,* and generally speaking in all pre-modern cultures, gifts were a kind of insurance. Kings gave out gifts to their subjects in order to ensure that when they really needed their subjects to step up (say in war or in the—it turns out—very likely event of a monster attack), those subjects would recall how readily they received treasures from their lords and do their part. And this exchange, of course, raises modern eyebrows. "Wait a minute," we say. "So the kings who gave stuff away weren't really any different from Scrooge or Heremod—just smarter. They were all just looking out for themselves, right? I mean, it's just as selfish to give stuff away so that people will stand by you when you need them as it is to refuse to give stuff away."

But that misses the point. It's not a question of being selfish or not; rather it's a question of having a happy human life within a society that functions as it should. And a happy society—where people are in dynamic and meaningful relationship with each other—is characterized by giving. When he receives treasures from King Hrothgar (which were themselves gifts to Hrothgar at some point), Beowulf goes home and straightaway gives them to his own liege-lord, King Hygelac. The point seems to be to keep treasure circulating as much as possible like blood being pumped by a heart. Beowulf and other Old English poems are unapologetic about their desire for treasures, because treasures and gifts are the furthest thing in the world from cold, hard cash or a number in a bank account. Instead, they are a glimmering symbol of communal life, intricately made and reflecting equally intricate layers of relationships and story.

Even shrewd giving—the kind recommended by the poem—is harder than keeping treasure for oneself because it requires trust. The people you give your stuff to may actually fail you in the day of battle, as Beowulf's own subjects do when he goes to fight a dragon in his old age and they chicken out. Or (to make this idea just a tad more applicable) others may not appreciate the gifts we give them. They may even take us for granted. And that is okay. The point is not that they appreciate it; the point is that they are worth it. The greater point, moreover, is that you have received more than you yourself can ever be properly thankful for. Everything you have is pure gift.

And so we celebrate Christmas over twelve days in order to learn to give and receive just a little better. If it's a spiritual discipline, it is not a very taxing one. Christmas becomes less about acquisition and more about this basic human activity, as we give and receive in the context of relationship, remembrance, and worship. Occasionally, we run out of gifts (it is twelve days, after all) and search for something else to give, an hour of quality time, a poem, a handicraft, an I.O.U., a song. And it matters what we give, but not as much as the giving or even the ability graciously to receive a better gift than we gave. Through it all, we are attending to each other, practicing gratitude and generosity, and rarely getting it quite perfect but coming nearer all the while to the Source.

There exists—in every moment—a shimmering web of gift, shining most intensely between family and friends but connecting all of humanity across all time and space and ultimately tying us back to the God who became Man at Christmas, who gave us all things, including himself, and who told us, "Freely you have received. Freely give."

ACTIVITIES

Reflect on the nature of the Trinity and have a conversation with a friend or community about how it operates, even if it's just to establish what some of your questions about it are. Keep in mind that this mystery has to do with the very essence of the Godhead and is ultimately impossible to understand completely, but the hints that we are given about the relationship at God's heart can be life-changing.

- Visit an old church or monastery, and spend time contemplating the nature of the Trinity and praying for the Church.
- Make a pastry in remembrance of Basil and Gregory (perhaps baklava), and share it with someone.
- Read part of a theology book (perhaps on the Trinity or the Holy Spirit), or begin to listen to a theology or church history podcast. (Wayne Grudem, C. S. Lewis, N. T. Wright, Miroslav Volf, Popes John Paul II and Benedict XVI, or Gregory and Basil themselves are all good places to start in figuring out why you believe what you believe).
- Listen to a podcast about Basil and Gregory, and write a short piece of historical fiction (or an epic poem) about their very eventful lives.

GIFT GIVING

- Give one of the gifts you did not give on the first day of Christmas.
- Give someone an icon or picture that will remind them of a theological truth, such as the Incarnation or Trinity.
- NO CASH OPTION: Find a way to serve someone in your community by doing the dishes, cooking dinner, or something else.

LITERATURE
"Huswifery" by Edward Taylor

Make me, O Lord, thy Spining Wheele compleate.
Thy Holy Worde my Distaff make for mee.
Make mine Affections thy Swift Flyers neate
And make my Soule thy holy Spoole to bee.
My Conversation make to be thy Reele
And reele the yarn thereon spun of thy Wheele.

Make me thy Loome then, knit therein this Twine:
And make thy Holy Spirit, Lord, winde quills:
Then weave the Web thyselfe. The yarn is fine.
Thine Ordinances make my Fulling Mills.
Then dy the same in Heavenly Colours Choice,
All pinkt with Varnisht Flowers of Paradise.

Then cloath therewith mine Understanding,
Will, Affections, Judgment, Conscience, Memory
My Words, and Actions, that their shine may fill
My wayes with glory and thee glorify.
Then mine apparell shall display before yee
That I am Cloathd in Holy robes for glory.

SCRIPTURE

Psalm 133, Ephesians 1:15–23, John 17:20–26

JOURNAL PROMPTS

How have giving and receiving gifts made you more vulnerable to people in your community and family this year? Have they made you more open to God?

What in your life do you hoard? And what is the difference between being ungenerous with others and maintaining healthy boundaries?
What gift have you enjoyed the most this year, so far?

How can you keep the treasures (material and immaterial) in your life circulating?

How can you continue to give generously in some way when the Christmas Season ends? Are there spiritual disciplines you can begin to observe that help you do this?

CAROLS

"Here We Come A-Wassailing"
"Dives and Lazarus"

The Tenth Day

It's still Christmas!

O God, in the course of this busy life, give us times of refreshment and peace; and grant that we may so use our leisure to rebuild our bodies and renew our minds, that our spirits may be opened to the goodness of your creation; through Jesus Christ our Lord. Amen.

—*The Book of Common Prayer*

REFLECTION

Does it still feel at all like Christmas to you? If you're like me, the answer is "No, not really." Most of us have gone back to work and have taken up habits that we think might help us live better this year. It is time for determination and action rather than contemplation or celebration. On December 24 or December 26, twelve whole days of Christmas might have seemed like a great idea. Now, it seems...out of step. It's time, instead, to get to work. To start the year off right. "Enough with the feasts," January seems to say. "Let's have some secular fasting."

I don't know if you've noticed, but there seems to be a different quality to the light itself now that we've reached January. The Christmas coziness and mystery, the fireplaces and bright lights-in-darkness have somehow given way, in a week's time, to something a bit more...gray. The days seem brighter, but not really in a cheerful way. I thought at first that maybe this had to do with Christmas lights being taken down, but when I look around, I notice that most are still up. This difference in the quality of light is really fascinating to me. I don't think there are two consecutive months that are more different than January and December, and the reason is not natural but cultural. Let's back up a moment and think about what this says about humans.

First, it says that my attitudes and experience of reality are far more culturally mediated than I care to acknowledge, even to myself. The weather itself looks different to me, despite the fact that I am still celebrating Christmas along with my family. Yet because December 25, along with January 1, has come and gone, something insistent within me—something connected to how most people around me are feeling and what they are doing—apprehends reality differently to the point that the very sky seems to have changed. Paradoxically, I am also hard-wired to resent this feeling, to fight against such conditioning, so that I can be "original" or "authentic" or "myself," whatever that means. (This hard-wiring, of course, is equally a product of the odd quirks in my own culture.)

But originality for originality's sake is actually rather pointless, besides being unachievable. The important thing is to harness and even embrace this tendency to be formed by our culture when it brings us into alignment with Reality, yet resisting the tendency when it destroys us. So yes, other people being "done" with Christmas affects my experience of the seasons, and that's fine, and even kind of cool.

But I want to do what I can to create, to contribute to, a culture where Christmas is less a month-long, commercial binge-with-a-climax to end the year (being to the year what a Saturday night party is to the working week) and more of a feast commencing after a long, prayerful fast, a twelve-day, uninterrupted feast that celebrates the Incarnation and both ends and begins the civic year. I want to do this partly because I think it will make my own life happier but also partly because I think it will enrich others' lives. I want to resist those aspects of our "Christmas social programming" that lead to long-term unhappiness, and I want to embrace those things that draw me closer to Christ and my neighbor.

This is also a time when we can affirm that Christmas really is about Christ and that drawing near to him is more important than feelings brought on by holly, the smell of nutmeg, twinkling, or jingling. It's more important than the lights of December, wonderful as they are. And if we continue to celebrate, we may well find the very thing to which all those bells and lights were bearing witness, deep beneath the gray January of the soul.

We think of fasting as being difficult and feasting as being easy. But it can be difficult to rejoice. Celebrating this tenth day of Christmas may feel wrong. It's secular Lent, after all: the time to make resolutions and make them come true, under our own steam. But celebration may be an act, not of gluttony and sloth, but of faith.

ACTIVITIES

- Don't forget to water your Christmas tree.
- Display Christmas cards on the refrigerator or wall, and take time to pray for the families/individuals who sent you the cards.
- Listen to some old-timey (very old-timey) Christmas carols. One of our favorite albums is Maddy Prior's *Carols at Christmas*.
- Play a board game with your family.
- Begin preparing for Twelfth Night; decide how you'd like to celebrate it.
- Sing a few Christmas carols, or have a Christmas carol dance party (interestingly enough, the word *carol* in its original sense implies dancing).
- Take a walk in a forest, by a river, or at the beach. Meditate on one of the Scriptures for the day.
- Watch a classic film with your family and talk about it afterwards.

GIFT GIVING

- If you have any left, give one of the gifts you did not give on the first day of Christmas. If you don't...
- Make someone a new winter hat, scarf, or coat out of old clothing you already have, and decorate it.
- NO CASH OPTION: Write a Christmas carol or poem about the person (take a cue from "Wassail, Wassail." Try to do better than mad-libbing "Rudolph the Red-Nosed Reindeer").

LITERATURE

"A Christmas Carol" by Samuel Taylor Coleridge

I
  The shepherds went their hasty way,
    And found the lowly stable-shed
  Where the Virgin-Mother lay:
    And now they checked their eager tread,
For to the Babe, that at her bosom clung,
A Mother's song the Virgin-Mother sung.

II
  They told her how a glorious light,
    Streaming from a heavenly throng.
  Around them shone, suspending night!
    While sweeter than a Mother's song,
Blest Angels heralded the Savior's birth,
Glory to God on high! and Peace on Earth.

III

   She listened to the tale divine,
      And closer still the Babe she pressed:
   And while she cried, the Babe is mine!
      The milk rushed faster to her breast:
Joy rose within her, like a summer's morn;
Peace, Peace on Earth! the Prince of Peace is born.

IV

   Thou Mother of the Prince of Peace,
      Poor, simple, and of low estate!
   That Strife should vanish, Battle cease,
      O why should this thy soul elate?
Sweet Music's loudest note, the Poet's story,
Didst thou ne'er love to hear of Fame and Glory?

V

   And is not War a youthful King,
      A stately Hero clad in Mail?
   Beneath his footsteps laurels spring;
      Him Earth's majestic monarchs hail
Their friends, their Playmate! and his bold bright eye
Compels the maiden's love-confessing sigh.

VI

   "Tell this in some more courtly scene,
      "To maids and youths in robes of state!
   "I am a woman poor and mean,
      "And therefore is my Soul elate.
"War is a ruffian, all with guilt defiled,
"That from the aged Father tears his Child!

VII

   "A murderous fiend, by fiends adored,
      "He kills the Sire and starves the Son;
   "The Husband kills, and from her board
      "Steals all his Widow's toil had won;
"Plunders God's world of beauty; rends away
"All safety from the Night, all comfort from the day.

VIII

   "Then wisely is my soul elate,
      "That strife should vanish, battle cease: ⸱
   "I'm poor and of low estate,
      "The Mother of the Prince of Peace.
"Joy rises in me, like a summer's morn:
"Peace, Peace on Earth! The Prince of Peace is born!

SCRIPTURE

Psalm 8, Ezra 8, John 2:1-12

JOURNAL PROMPTS

Do you feel different today from how you felt on December 24th?
What about December 27th? Why or why not?

How can you (or should you) resist the way secular culture celebrates
Christmas (and New Year's, for that matter)?

How can feasting actually become a spiritual discipline? When is
celebration difficult, and how do we overcome this difficulty?

CAROLS

"Joy to the World"
"Joseph and Mary (The Cherry Tree Carol)"

The Eleventh Day

Feasts of St. Simeon Stylites, St. Elizabeth Seton

Almighty God our heavenly Father, you declare your glory and show forth your handiwork in the heavens and in the earth: Deliver us in our various occupations from the service of self alone, that we may do the work you give us to do in truth and beauty and for the common good; for the sake of him who came among us as one who serves, your Son Jesus Christ our Lord, who lives and reigns with you and the Holy Spirit, one God, for ever and ever. Amen.

—*The Book of Common Prayer*

REFLECTION

The Western Church today celebrates the life and ministry of Simeon Stylites (390?-459) who stayed on top of a pillar for 37 years, praying, preaching, and practicing extreme asceticism in what is now Syria. This is a pretty appropriate feast to celebrate on the day preceding topsy-turvy Twelfth Night, so I thought I'd say a few words about it here.

The easiest response to St. Simeon's story is skepticism—not that he stayed atop a pillar for all that time (unlike Thoreau at Walden, he had plenty of witnesses), but that such an activity has anything to do with real holiness. It's all a bit vulgar, and we prefer the well-mannered saint who preaches the gospel quietly, through kindness to others, without condemning and without anger. If Simeon was really that holy, we might think, he would be a tad more like St. Francis of Assisi or maybe George MacDonald. You just don't go and sit on the top of a pillar out in the desert by yourself out of pure motives, do you? Can't we just dismiss this brand of sanctity the way we dismiss Father Ferapont in *The Brothers Karamazov* or those billboards about how Saturday is the true Lord's Day?

The problem is that skepticism rarely does much to help our souls, unless it's in the service of truth. It's possible, of course, that Simeon was crazy or a hypocrite (I doubt it myself—you just don't commit to something like staying on the top of a pillar for 37 years without presence of mind and some level of discipline). He was probably, at the very least, off-putting. But even if he was a crazy old coot or a showoff, believing that doesn't really challenge me to live my life any differently or help me to grow. Skepticism is useful when it allows us to see truth behind misperception so that we may align ourselves with that truth, but it's not really useful as an automatic response, a philosophy, or a defense mechanism. Beware of smirks.

Such an attitude to over-the-top holiness disregards as well Jesus' commendation of John the Baptist. The prophet who stayed out in the desert eating locusts and honey (shouting "Repent!" all the time) and baptizing people in the Jordan had a very different personality and ministry from Jesus', but his way of doing things was actually quite necessary. There is a passage in Matthew 11 where Jesus contrasts his ministry to John's. Not once does Jesus claim that his own seemingly less severe method of ministry is superior to that of the Baptizer: "John came neither eating nor drinking and you say, 'He has a demon'; the son of man came both eating and drinking, and you say, 'Here is a drunkard and a glutton, who hangs out with tax collectors and sinners.'" People tend to get annoyed with the truth because it's uncomfortable, and they reach for whatever excuses they can find to discredit those who preach it. Of course, John's or Simeon's "feats of saintly strength" are not the point here. What they do, instead, is "prepare the way" for Christ by getting people's attention so that God's love and grace can be administered to repentant sinners through the good news of God's Kingdom.

We're drawing near in the calendar, now, to the end of Christmas and the beginning of Epiphany. The one season celebrates the coming to earth of Christ; the other celebrates how he was revealed as Lamb of God and King, both to the foreign Magi, and to John the Baptist's followers. The strangeness of the signs themselves—of John, called the "burning and shining lamp," or of the Star—somehow prepares the way for us to see God in a new way. But we cannot dull ourselves with cynicism; instead, we must desire, and practice seeing, the grace of God at work in the strangest things. Begin to ask God to manifest his grace to you through the lives of others—even those lives you're tempted to dismiss, even the supposed hypocrites and weirdos. Showing them grace, you might be surprised at the way that same grace spills over to allow you to recognize Christ: at the revelation of God that grips your own heart and makes it free.

ACTIVITIES

- Pray in a tree for an hour in memory of St. Simeon Stylites!
- Read a book in memory of St. Elizabeth Ann Seton.
- Take a walk in a cemetery and ponder mortality.
- Look back over some of the previous days' suggested activities that you wanted to do, and do them now!
- Use social media with the express intent to bless someone else (rather than to "consume" or be entertained).
- Three words: Feats of Strength.
- Listen to some old-timey Christmas/Twelfth Night carols.
- Read about the current persecution of Christians occurring in Syria and find a way to help. Pray for all the people of Syria.
- Invite people to a Twelfth Night party tomorrow!

GIFT GIVING

- Give a small donation to a Christian/Catholic school you support in memory of St. Elizabeth Ann Seton.
- Think about something that makes someone in your life eccentric or extraordinary, and give a gift that reflects this aspect of them (without insulting them).
- NO CASH OPTION: Write down eleven of your favorite things about someone, and give them the list.

LITERATURE

"St. Simeon Stylites" by Alfred, Lord Tennyson

Altho' I be the basest of mankind,
From scalp to sole one slough and crust of sin,
Unfit for earth, unfit for heaven, scarce meet
For troops of devils, mad with blasphemy,
I will not cease to grasp the hope I hold
Of saintdom, and to clamour, morn and sob,
Battering the gates of heaven with storms of prayer,
Have mercy, Lord, and take away my sin.
Let this avail, just, dreadful, mighty God,
This not be all in vain that thrice ten years,
Thrice multiplied by superhuman pangs,
In hungers and in thirsts, fevers and cold,
In coughs, aches, stitches, ulcerous throes and cramps,
A sign betwixt the meadow and the cloud,
Patient on this tall pillar I have borne
Rain, wind, frost, heat, hail, damp, and sleet, and snow;
And I had hoped that ere this period closed
Thou wouldst have caught me up into Thy rest,
Denying not these weather-beaten limbs
The meed of saints, the white robe and the palm.
O take the meaning, Lord: I do not breathe,
Not whisper, any murmur of complaint.
Pain heap'd ten-hundred-fold to this, were still
Less burthen, by ten-hundred-fold, to bear,
Than were those lead-like tons of sin, that crush'd
My spirit flat before thee. O Lord, Lord,
Thou knowest I bore this better at the first,
For I was strong and hale of body then;
And tho' my teeth, which now are dropt away,
Would chatter with the cold, and all my beard
Was tagg'd with icy fringes in the moon,
I drown'd the whoopings of the owl with sound
Of pious hymns and psalms, and sometimes saw
An angel stand and watch me, as I sang.

Now am I feeble grown; my end draws nigh;
I hope my end draws nigh: half deaf I am,
So that I scarce can hear the people hum
About the column's base, and almost blind,
And scarce can recognise the fields I know;
And both my thighs are rotted with the dew;
Yet cease I not to clamour and to cry,
While my stiff spine can hold my weary head,
Till all my limbs drop piecemeal from the stone,
Have mercy, mercy: take away my sin.
O Jesus, if thou wilt not save my soul,
Who may be saved? who is it may be saved?
Who may be made a saint, if I fail here?
Show me the man hath suffered more than I.
For did not all thy martyrs die one death?
For either they were stoned, or crucified,
Or burn'd in fire, or boil'd in oil, or sawn
In twain beneath the ribs; but I die here
To-day, and whole years long, a life of death.
Bear witness, if I could have found a way
(And heedfully I sifted all my thought)
More slowly-painful to subdue this home
Of sin, my flesh, which I despise and hate,
I had not stinted practice, O my God.
For not alone this pillar-punishment,
Not this alone I bore: but while I lived
In the white convent down the valley there,
For many weeks about my loins I wore
The rope that haled the buckets from the well,
Twisted as tight as I could knot the noose;
And spake not of it to a single soul,
Until the ulcer, eating thro' my skin,
Betray'd my secret penance, so that all
My brethren marvell'd greatly. More than this
I bore, whereof, O God, thou knowest all.
Three winters, that my soul might grow to thee,
I lived up there on yonder mountain side.
My right leg chain'd into the crag, I lay

Pent in a roofless close of ragged stones;
Inswathed sometimes in wandering mist, and twice
Black'd with thy branding thunder, and sometimes
Sucking the damps for drink, and eating not,
Except the spare chance-gift of those that came
To touch my body and be heal'd, and live:
And they say then that I work'd miracles,
Whereof my fame is loud amongst mankind,
Cured lameness, palsies, cancers. Thou, O God,
Knowest alone whether this was or no.
Have mercy, mercy; cover all my sin.
Then, that I might be more alone with thee,
Three years I lived upon a pillar, high
Six cubits, and three years on one of twelve;
And twice three years I crouch'd on one that rose
Twenty by measure; last of all, I grew
Twice ten long weary weary years to this,
That numbers forty cubits from the soil.
I think that I have borne as much as this—
Or else I dream--and for so long a time,
If I may measure time by yon slow light,
And this high dial, which my sorrow crowns—
So much—even so. And yet I know not well,
For that the evil ones come here, and say,
"Fall down, O Simeon: thou hast suffer'd long
For ages and for ages!" Then they prate
Of penances I cannot have gone thro',
Perplexing me with lies; and oft I fall,
Maybe for months, in such blind lethargies,
That Heaven, and Earth, and Time are choked. But yet
Bethink thee, Lord, while thou and all the saints
Enjoy themselves in Heaven, and men on earth
House in the shade of comfortable roofs,
Sit with their wives by fires, eat wholesome food,
And wear warm clothes, and even beasts have stalls,
I, 'tween the spring and downfall of the light,
Bow down one thousand and two hundred times,
To Christ, the Virgin Mother, and the Saints;

Or in the night, after a little sleep,
I wake: the chill stars sparkle; I am wet
With drenching dews, or stiff with crackling frost.
I wear an undress'd goatskin on my back;
A grazing iron collar grinds my neck;
And in my weak, lean arms I lift the cross,
And strive and wrestle with thee till I die:
O mercy, mercy! wash away my sin.
O Lord, thou knowest what a man I am;
A sinful man, conceived and born in sin:
'Tis their own doing; this is none of mine;
Lay it not to me. Am I to blame for this,
That here come those that worship me? Ha! ha!
They think that I am somewhat. What am I?
The silly people take me for a saint,
And bring me offerings of fruit and flowers:
And I, in truth (thou wilt bear witness here)
Have all in all endured as much, and more
Than many just and holy men, whose names
Are register'd and calendar'd for saints.
Good people, you do ill to kneel to me.
What is it I can have done to merit this?
I am a sinner viler than you all.
It may be I have wrought some miracles,
And cured some halt and maim'd; but what of that?
It may be, no one, even among the saints,
May match his pains with mine; but what of that?
Yet do not rise: for you may look on me,
And in your looking you may kneel to God.
Speak! is there any of you halt or maim'd?
I think you know I have some power with Heaven
From my long penance: let him speak his wish.
Yes, I can heal. Power goes forth from me.
They say that they are heal'd. Ah, hark! they shout
"St. Simeon Stylites". Why, if so,
God reaps a harvest in me. O my soul,
God reaps a harvest in thee. If this be,
Can I work miracles and not be saved?

This is not told of any. They were saints.
It cannot be but that I shall be saved;
Yea, crown'd a saint. They shout, "Behold a saint!"
And lower voices saint me from above.
Courage, St. Simeon! This dull chrysalis
Cracks into shining wings, and hope ere death
Spreads more and more and more, that God hath now
Sponged and made blank of crimeful record all
My mortal archives. O my sons, my sons,
I, Simeon of the pillar, by surname Stylites, among men;
I, Simeon, the watcher on the column till the end;
I, Simeon, whose brain the sunshine bakes;
I, whose bald brows in silent hours become
Unnaturally hoar with rime, do now
From my high nest of penance here proclaim
That Pontius and Iscariot by my side
Show'd like fair seraphs. On the coals I lay,
A vessel full of sin: all hell beneath
Made me boil over. Devils pluck'd my sleeve;
Abaddon and Asmodeus caught at me.
I smote them with the cross; they swarm'd again.
In bed like monstrous apes they crush'd my chest:
They flapp'd my light out as I read: I saw
Their faces grow between me and my book:
With colt-like whinny and with hoggish whine
They burst my prayer. Yet this way was left,
And by this way I'scaped them. Mortify
Your flesh, like me, with scourges and with thorns;
Smite, shrink not, spare not. If it may be, fast
Whole Lents, and pray. I hardly, with slow steps,
With slow, faint steps, and much exceeding pain,
Have scrambled past those pits of fire, that still
Sing in mine ears. But yield not me the praise:
God only thro' his bounty hath thought fit,
Among the powers and princes of this world,
To make me an example to mankind,

Which few can reach to. Yet I do not say
But that a time may come—yea, even now,
Now, now, his footsteps smite the threshold stairs
Of life—I say, that time is at the doors
When you may worship me without reproach;
For I will leave my relics in your land,
And you may carve a shrine about my dust,
And burn a fragrant lamp before my bones,
When I am gather'd to the glorious saints.
While I spake then, a sting of shrewdest pain
Ran shrivelling thro' me, and a cloudlike change,
In passing, with a grosser film made thick
These heavy, horny eyes. The end! the end!
Surely the end! What's here? A shape, a shade,
A flash of light. Is that the angel there
That holds a crown? Come, blessed brother, come,
I know thy glittering face. I waited long;
My brows are ready. What! Deny it now?
Nay, draw, draw, draw nigh. So I clutch it. Christ!
'Tis gone: 'tis here again; the crown! The crown!
So now 'tis fitted on and grows to me,
And from it melt the dews of Paradise,
Sweet! Sweet! Spikenard, and balm, and frankincense.
Ah! let me not be fool'd, sweet saints: I trust
That I am whole, and clean, and meet for Heaven.
Speak, if there be a priest, a man of God,
Among you there, and let him presently
Approach, and lean a ladder on the shaft,
And climbing up into my airy home,
Deliver me the blessed sacrament;
For by the warning of the Holy Ghost,
I prophesy that I shall die to-night,
A quarter before twelve. But thou, O Lord,
Aid all this foolish people; let them take
Example, pattern: lead them to thy light.

SCRIPTURE

Psalm 11, Matthew 11:2-30

JOURNAL PROMPTS

What is one of the strangest, most counterintuitive ways you've seen God work?

How is God calling you to bear witness to him in uncomfortable ways?

When do we find holiness distasteful? Why? How is this different from disliking the eccentricity of holy people?

CAROLS

"While Shepherds Watched Their Flock by Night"
"Go Tell it on the Mountain"

Sacred to Love.

TWELFTH NIGHT.

1 queer set was assembled.   To the left of my Lord a

The Twelfth Day

The Twelfth Night

Father in heaven, who at the baptism of Jesus in the River Jordan proclaimed him your beloved Son and anointed him with the Holy Spirit: Grant that all who are baptized into his Name may keep the covenant they have made, and boldly confess him as Lord and Savior; who with you and the Holy Spirit lives and reigns, one God, in glory everlasting.

—*The Book of Common Prayer*

REFLECTION

Shakespeare wrote a play called *Twelfth Night,* and it follows the basic pattern of most of his comedies. The pattern tends to run like this: In Part One, there is a normal state of affairs that is not ideal—a duke or king has been usurped or lovers are not allowed to be married. In Part Two, everything is turned even more upside-down for a brief period of time as certain characters don disguises, become enchanted, or get lost. In Part Three, a revelation occurs—an epiphany—that dispels the disguise or enchantment and resolves not only the problems from Part Two but also the long existing problems in Part One. The world in which the play exists is cleansed, orderly, and joyful by the end; truth, charity, and justice have triumphed, and the actors take a bow. I have a theory that Shakespeare, who would have grown up celebrating Twelfth Night—a night of partying and topsy-turviness inherited from medieval traditions—had this pattern baked into his soul. Part of the reason his comedies so resonated with his first audience was that they were also quite familiar with the structure of these celebrations.

The Twelfth Night—Epiphany Eve—feast was usually the high point of the Christmas season, and it featured a lot of drinking, eating, and caroling, as well as the inversion of the normal order of things. Landowners did menial work (such as turning spits), and anyone who came to the feast could be appointed "Lord of Misrule," directing the night's revels and bossing everyone around for an evening.

Mikhail Bakhtin, a 20th-Century Russian critic, developed a theory about how these topsy-turvy feasts worked in the Middle Ages just before Shakespeare's time. He reasoned that things were so rigidly structured in terms of hierarchy, class, and dogma during the medieval period that such festivities acted as a kind of "pressure valve" to keep the common people from rebelling against their lords. They had a "carnivalesque" night of revelry a few times a year, and that kept them compliant for the next few months, as they slaved away for "the Man" or the Church, or whomever. I know, I know—leave it to a literary critic to turn fun into functional. This is still a pretty popular way to interpret these celebrations, and it does reflect some of the statements made (at least by monks) at the time (the *Tudor Monastery Farm* folks interpret it this way as well in what is a fantastic documentary).

I'm not convinced by Bakhtin's theory, though, and I'll tell you why. No one really hates order itself. Even in societies far more rigid than medieval England (for instance, Shakespeare's England or Bakhtin's USSR), it is not order and hierarchy we mind so much as someone else's imperfect order and hierarchy being imposed on us. The fact is that, whether our society is a well-oiled machine or positively anarchic, it is just part of a crazy, topsy-turvy world where we often feel helpless before chaotic forces that we can't control. There certainly is beauty and order in this world, but in nature, in social structures, and in our hearts, there is a lot of disorder, too. In a restrictive and hierarchical society, organization itself isn't bad until it is used to enforce chaotic injustice.

The world, in other words, is always upside-down. It's part of the reason that the play *Twelfth Night* still resonates with people who have never even heard of the feast it is named after. Yet the feast and the comedies both dramatize the same thing: the fact that the world is already a pretty crazy place and that all structures have a bit of the chaotic about them, a bit of the arbitrary. Injustice often prevails in this world; bad people are often rich and good people poor; society commends as virtuous the things that are vile and forces its inverted standards upon others; sacrifice and honest achievement are met with ingratitude and envy; and real need is often answered not with charity but glib self-satisfaction. It has always been this way, yet we should mourn our own part in this mess.

In a way, then, to enjoy an upside-down feast (whether this be Twelfth Night or the practice of Twelvetide itself) is not so much releasing pressure so that the peasants don't rise up this year as it is telling the truth about ourselves and our society. But in a way, it is also wishing for, and delighting in, a new kind of order that may on its face feel like disorder. The Son of Man came both eating and drinking, and the Pharisees, who took themselves as seriously as Shakespeare's Malvolio in *Twelfth Night*, said, "Look, a glutton and a drunkard!" Yet this seeming chaos that attended Christ and his followers who "turned the world upside-down" brought true Order to multitudes, starting with their hearts. That's not to say we give our minds and souls up to the chaos, that we stop fighting it to indulge the flesh or the ego. It is to say that we rejoice, that we refuse our own petty refusal of joy.

Because, of course, there must be a real Order we are waiting for. If there wasn't, the false sorts of order–the chaos masquerading as structure—wouldn't feel like such a betrayal. It is when the True King shows up and doffs his carnival disguise that the false kings are revealed as false. But of course it wouldn't be so satisfying if we didn't already know the old king fell short of what a King was supposed to look like. We would not be distressed by counterfeits if, deep down, we didn't know about the real thing.

This is why the inversions of Twelfth Night precede Epiphany. Not merely a reversal of Carnivalesque Misrule, Revelation is rather its culmination. Christ revealed himself first to those who joined his odd little band of misfits and outcasts. It is in the mess of Twelfth Night, when we are no longer righteous in our own eyes, that God may begin to fill our vision in new ways, to draw us up to the true Feast, of which the best worldly revelry, as well as the best worldly rule, is only a shadow.

So the kings draw closer to the King, and the wise approach Wisdom Himself. They are dethroned and made into fools, but it is only thus that they can enter into their Master's joy.

ACTIVITIES

Have a Twelfth Night party with your family or community. Sing some of the carols suggested at the end of the section and do some of the below activities.

- Drink some cider or wassail and go wassailing, as is traditional on Twelfth Night. A thousand recipes for wassail can be found in an online search.
- Have a white elephant gift exchange with friends/family.
- Draw straws to find out who is going to be the "Lord/Lady of Misrule" for the day (more fun if it's a child), and waste the day following their suggestions. Alternatively (as is more traditional), bake a cake with a dried pea in it. Whoever gets the pea presides over the evening's Twelfth Night festivities.
- Today and tomorrow, do a variation of "Elf on the Shelf" with nativity Wise Men, as they journey to Bethlehem.
- Watch Shakespeare's *Twelfth Night* with friends. You can find various versions on YouTube. Or read the play with friends, assigning parts.
- Plant your Christmas tree in the backyard, or else retire it with honors, maybe singing "O Tannenbaum" as a dirge with the lyrics changed to past tense.

GIFT GIVING

- Give one of the larger gifts that you did not give at Christmas.
- Give to an organization that serves the poor in someone's name, in order to remember St. John Nepomucene Neuman, whose feast is also celebrated on this day.
- NO CASH OPTION: Give someone a "white elephant gift" (hopefully in the context of an exchange where the other person is cued in to the fact that you are not giving each other serious presents).

LITERATURE

From Twelfth Night *by William Shakespeare*

An excerpt from Act 2, Scene 3, of Shakespeare's comedy. Three of the comic ("low") characters are celebrating Twelfth Night together by getting good and drunk when Malvolio, the steward of Lady Olivia's household, takes them to task.

[Enter MARIA]

MARIA. What a caterwauling do you keep here! If my lady have not called up her steward Malvolio and bid him turn you out of doors, never trust me.

SIR TOBY BELCH My lady's a Cataian, we are politicians, Malvolio's a Peg-a-Ramsey, and 'Three merry men be we.' Am not I consanguineous? Am I not of her blood? Tillyvally. Lady!

[Sings]

'There dwelt a man in Babylon, lady, lady!'

FESTE Beshrew me, the knight's in admirable fooling.

SIR ANDREW AGUECHEEK Ay, he does well enough if he be disposed, and so do I too: he does it with a better grace, but I do it more natural.

SIR TOBY BELCH [Sings] 'O, the twelfth day of December,' –

MARIA For the love o' God, peace!

[Enter MALVOLIO]

MALVOLIO My masters, are you mad? or what are you? Have ye no wit, manners, nor honesty, but to gabble like tinkers at this time of night? Do ye make an alehouse of my lady's house, that ye squeak out your coziers' catches without any mitigation or remorse of voice? Is there no respect of place, persons, nor time in you?

SIR TOBY BELCH We did keep time, sir, in our catches. Sneck up!

MALVOLIO Sir Toby, I must be round with you. My lady bade me tell you, that, though she harbours you as her kinsman, she's nothing allied to your disorders. If you can separate yourself and your misdemeanors, you are welcome to the house; if not, an it would please you to take leave of her, she is very willing to bid you farewell.

SIR TOBY BELCH 'Farewell, dear heart, since I must needs be gone.'
MARIA Nay, good Sir Toby.
FESTE 'His eyes do show his days are almost done.'
MALVOLIO Is't even so?
SIR TOBY BELCH 'But I will never die.'
FESTE Sir Toby, there you lie.
MALVOLIO This is much credit to you.
Sir Toby Belch. 'Shall I bid him go?'
FESTE 'What an if you do?'
SIR TOBY BELCH 'Shall I bid him go, and spare not?'
FESTE 'O no, no, no, no, you dare not.'
SIR TOBY BELCH Out o' tune, sir: ye lie. Art any more than
a steward? Dost thou think, because thou art virtuous, there shall be no
more cakes and ale?
FESTE Yes, by Saint Anne, and ginger shall be hot i' the mouth too.
SIR TOBY BELCH Thou'rt i' the right. Go, sir, rub your chain
with crumbs. A stoup of wine, Maria!
MALVOLIO Mistress Mary, if you prized my lady's favour at any thing
more than contempt, you would not give means for this uncivil rule: she
shall know of it, by this hand. [Exit]
MARIA Go shake your ears.
SIR ANDREW AGUECHEEK 'Twere as good a deed as to drink when
a man's a-hungry, to challenge him the field, and then to break promise
with him and make a fool of him.
SIR TOBY BELCH Do't, knight: I'll write thee a challenge: or
I'll deliver thy indignation to him by word of mouth.
MARIA Sweet Sir Toby, be patient for tonight: since the youth of the
count's was today with thy lady, she is much out of quiet. For Monsieur
Malvolio, let me alone with him: if I do not gull him into a nayword,
and make him a common recreation, do not think I have wit enough to
lie straight in my bed: I know I can do it.
SIR TOBY BELCH Possess us, possess us; tell us something of him.
MARIA Marry, sir, sometimes he is a kind of puritan.
SIR ANDREW AGUECHEEK O, if I thought that I'd beat him like a
dog!
SIR TOBY BELCH What, for being a puritan? Thy exquisite

reason, dear knight?

SIR ANDREW AGUECHEEK I have no exquisite reason for't, but I have reason good enough.

MARIA The devil a puritan that he is, or any thing constantly, but a time-pleaser; an affectioned ass, that cons state without book and utters it by great swarths: the best persuaded of himself, so crammed, as he thinks, with excellencies, that it is his grounds of faith that all that look on him love him; and on that vice in him will my revenge find notable cause to work.

SIR TOBY BELCH What wilt thou do?

MARIA I will drop in his way some obscure epistles of love; wherein, by the colour of his beard, the shape of his leg, the manner of his gait, the expressure of his eye, forehead, and complexion, he shall find himself most feelingly personated. I can write very like my lady your niece: on a forgotten matter we can hardly make distinction of our hands.

SIR TOBY BELCH Excellent! I smell a device.

SIR ANDREW AGUECHEEK I have't in my nose too.

SIR TOBY BELCH He shall think, by the letters that thou wilt drop, that they come from my niece, and that she's in love with him.

MARIA My purpose is, indeed, a horse of that colour.

SIR ANDREW AGUECHEEK And your horse now would make him an ass.

MARIA Ass, I doubt not.

SIR ANDREW AGUECHEEK O, 'twill be admirable!

MARIA Sport royal, I warrant you: I know my physic will work with him. I will plant you two, and let the fool make a third, where he shall find the letter: observe his construction of it. For this night, to bed, and dream on the event. Farewell. [Exit]

SIR TOBY BELCH Good night, Penthesilea.

SIR ANDREW AGUECHEEK Before me, she's a good wench.

SIR TOBY BELCH She's a beagle, true-bred, and one that adores me: what o' that?

SIR ANDREW AGUECHEEK I was adored once too.

SIR TOBY BELCH Let's to bed, knight. Thou hadst need send for more money.

SIR ANDREW AGUECHEEK. If I cannot recover your niece, I am a foul way out.

SIR TOBY BELCH Send for money, knight: if thou hast her not i' the end, call me cut.

SIR ANDREW AGUECHEEK If I do not, never trust me, take it how you will.

SIR TOBY BELCH Come, come, I'll go burn some sack; 'tis too late to go to bed now: come, knight; come, knight. [Exit]

This prompts the comic sub-plot of the play, which will result in Malvolio becoming more absurd as he grows infatuated with Lady Olivia, thanks to forged love-notes. The entire play, by virtue of its title and setting, is an obvious choice for Twelfth Night and Epiphany, especially because it deals with a temporary reversal (or confusion) of order followed by an unmasking/ revelation. The scene is appropriate because it mocks the two opposite (and rather silly) extreme reactions to Christmas celebrations: dissipation, on the one hand, and prudish refusal to have fun on the other.

Not bad, Shakespeare. Not bad at all.

SCRIPTURE

Jonah, Matthew 3

JOURNAL PROMPTS

How can you refuse your refusal of joy?

What are the things in your life that still seem disordered?
Write them out and ask God not only to order them but to give you a
revelation of Himself.

What is the relationship between revelry and joy?

If all social structures are in some way unjust, when should the
Christian favor overturning them and starting over?
Keep in mind that the social structure that replaces it will likewise be
imperfect (until Christ's return).

CAROLS

"Gloucestershire Wassail"
"The Boar's Head Carol"
"The Holly and the Ivy"

The Epiphany

O God, by the leading of a star you manifested your only Son to the peoples of the earth: Lead us, who know you now by faith, to your presence, where we may see your glory face to face; through Jesus Christ our Lord, who lives and reigns with you and the Holy Spirit, one God, now and for ever. Amen.

—*The Book of Common Prayer*

REFLECTION

It is never something that God owes us. We could fast in the desert for thirty years or journey over field and fountain, moor and mountain. The epiphany of God to Jew and Gentile alike is grace. It is gift.

This gift prompts answering gift. The wise men to whom Christ's star is revealed in the heavens bring precious gold, frankincense, and myrrh. The one who shook Elizabeth's womb also recognizes Christ as an adult, hears the words "Behold, the Lamb of God who takes away the sins of the world!" coming out of his own mouth as he suddenly comprehends (enough of) Christ's identity and mission, and gives as gift his own ministry in response: "He must increase. I must decrease."

Implicit in a true revelation of God, always, is a revelation of God's generosity to us. And that generosity at the heart of God, manifested first in the Trinity itself and second in his provision for his creatures, inspires those created in his image to give as freely as they have received. He was perfectly entitled, again, to keep himself to himself. And so are we. Dependent, incomplete beings though we are, he gives most of us the option to pretend we do not owe anything to anyone.

But he also gives us the option to exchange gifts with himself, with Almighty God.

I do not know how to do this well. Do I try, stumblingly, without feeling or satisfaction, awkwardly to give to other people? Do I wait on God, praying that he will manifest himself to me in such a way that I cannot help but give myself? Perhaps both? And what of judgment, of my being called to account for what I have not given, what I have not done? How can we give freely, image forth God's kindness, if we mainly do so in fear of being cast into the outer darkness? "I knew you to be a hard man, master...."

One of the weirdest things I sometimes see parents do is expect small children to be grateful but then become offended or laugh and say, "Look at how ungrateful they are," when kids are given things and act like jerks about it. We still deal with this with one or two of our kids during a few of the days of Christmas each year. And sometimes it's hilarious.

But because they won't always be three, and ingratitude won't always be cute, we've gotten in the habit of saying things like, "Now, we're going to give you something today that is not a toy. You still need to say, 'Thank you, Mommy and Daddy.'" We've never been romantic enough about child-rearing to expect the little creatures that emerged from us to be naturally grateful about anything. We're not (by this point) surprised when they act like ingrates despite our best efforts to give them the world. But the more we've corrected this behavior and taught them to say grateful things (occasionally through threat of punishment), the more their responses have approached something that seems close to actual gratitude. But it's a habit—first of behavior, then of mind—that we've had to inculcate. And we do it, not because we need their good behavior, but because it makes them happier people in the long-run.

I can't easily answer the question about judgment I've posed above. But I wonder if one way to approach it isn't simply to practice gratefulness when possible, even when uninspired: to mouth the right words and ask God's mercy when our hearts are far from feeling grateful. I wonder if the deliberate spiritual discipline of thanking God–of making yourself thank

God–might not inculcate gradual epiphany.

Because the amazing thing is that though we usually do not recognize it, really all we have in this life is a gift—each moment a bright box brimming over with revelation of God. It is our task to learn to view each season, each day, each hour, and each present moment—however painful or pleasurable—as both pure Gift and Word. We must train ourselves to participate in the epiphany that has already been provided. If we can train our children to practice gratitude (with their faltering help), perhaps God can even train us (with ours).

Happy Epiphany!

GIFT GIVING

- Ask your children (or yourself) to think of three gifts they can give to Christ today or over the next year.

ACTIVITIES

- Celebrate Epiphany by making use of any of the traditions around the world, from dressing as the three wise men and going door-to-door singing carols to baking a King Cake to giving gifts.
- Read the account in Matthew 2 and have your children draw a picture of the Magi bringing gifts to the house in Bethlehem. Note that in the narrative the exact number of wisemen isn't given, there is a house (rather than a stable) involved, and the event seems to be about two years after Jesus' birth.
- Take down your Christmas decorations today.
- Thank someone else for something they've done for you over the past year (or years) that you've tended to take for granted.

LITERATURE
"Lo" by Chris Pipkin

God comes in flesh, disguised and yet displayed
in Virgin, Manger, River, Mount, and Tomb.
We saw him in the places where he stayed
yet did not see. We served but made no room.
We sang and gave and feasted, and we prayed
and passed the time in golds and reds and greens.
We were, perhaps, relieved, when it was done,
to turn our hands to clocks, our eyes to screens:
A child is born, and, mostly, we had fun.
The Fact is there, whatever else it means.
Yet deeper than God's deeds, his graces run—
they grant a Recognition, without Whom
all gifts remain unwrapped behind the tree.
Christ's crowning kindness is Epiphany.

SCRIPTURE

Genesis 6, Isaiah 6, Psalm 96,
Ephesians 1:15-23, Matthew 2:1-12

JOURNAL PROMPTS

Why do you think God revealed Jesus to pagan astrologers?

What are some ways you can train yourself to be grateful until it becomes a natural response?

What is a gift God is giving you right now that you only just recognized?

How does Epiphany (recognition) complete Christmas (God's giving of Himself to us)?

CAROLS

"We Three Kings"
"This Endris Night"

OUR FAMILY TRADITIONS

*Write some of your family traditions around Christmas
or ideas for new traditions here.*

_____

_____

_____

_____

_____

_____

_____

_____

_____

_____

_____

_____

_____

_____

If you benefited from this book in any way, please consider giving it a five-star rating on Amazon. This will help us enormously, and it will also help this type of Christmas celebration to catch on.

To subscribe to our mailing list, visit 12tide.com and opt in on the homepage.

We'd also love to hear from you. Feel free to email us at dozendaysofchristmas@gmail.com with suggestions and thoughts.

As always, check out the site, **12tide.com,** for even more Christmas (and Advent) resources.

Finally, if you'd like to take a look at some other things we've been up to (besides working jobs and raising kids), feel free to check out the following:

Chris' podcast, The Inklings Variety Hour, which can be found on Apple, Stitcher, Google Podcasts and more.

Glencora's design business, pipkincreative.com

See you next Twelvetide!

Made in United States
Orlando, FL
20 November 2024

54146988R10095